Look, Learn & Create

Polymer Clay

A WORKSHOP
101
IN A BOOK

Creative Publishing
international

Quarto is the authority on a wide range of topics.

Quarto educates, entertains and enriches the lives of our readers—enthusiasts and lovers of hands-on living.

www.QuartoKnows.com

Copyright © 2011, Quarto Publishing Group USA Inc.
This paperback edition published in 2017
First published in the United States of America in 2011 by
Creative Publishing international, Inc.,
an imprint of Quarto Publishing Group USA Inc.
400 First Avenue North, Suite 400
Minneapolis, Minnesota 55401
1-800-328-3895
QuartoKnows.com
Visit our blogs at QuartoKnows.com

ISBN13: 978-1-58923-470-3
Printed in USA

Library of Congress Cataloging-in-Publication Data

Mabray, Angela.
  Polymer clay 101 / Angela Mabray and
Kim Otterbein.
      p. cm.
  Includes index.
  Summary: "Beginner's guide to crafting with polymer
clay, teaching all the basic techniques through easy
projects.
  ISBN-13: 978-1-58923-470-3 (hard cover)
  ISBN-10: 1-58923-470-7 (hard cover)
  1. Polymer clay craft. I. Otterbein, Kim. II. Title.

  TT297.M22 2011
  738.1'2--dc22

2010016772

Photographers: Corean Komarec, Angela Mabray,
  Jeffrey Otterbein
Photo Coordinator: Joanne Wawra
Copy Editor: Ellen Goldstein
Cover & Book Design: Mighty Media, Inc.
Page Layout: Mighty Media, Inc.
Videographer: Tanner Herriott

Acknowledgments

Thanks to the online polymer clay community for the many things they've taught me and for the many friends I've made. Without them, there would be so much more error to my trial and error! Thanks to the Central Oklahoma Polymer Clay Guild for helping me stretch beyond my comfort zone. Thanks to Christi Friesen for her giving personality and for her role in making this book happen. I am grateful beyond words to my family for believing in me. And most of all, thanks to Billy for the adventures!

—Angela

I'd like to thank my husband, Jeff, for being the cameraman and being the best clay conditioning "machine" on the east coast. Also, I'd like to thank Pamela Cole for helping me with the text.

—Kim

CONTENTS

Introduction

Like many artists, I had heard about polymer clay, but had a lot of other crafts in my life, and wasn't sure I had time for another one. Then I saw a very shiny, perfectly round bangle bracelet. When I looked closer, I saw tiny designs and intricate patterns throughout the bangle. The bracelet was beautiful. I thought, "This is made out of polymer clay? Amazing!"

Inspired by what I had seen, I bought just a few colors of clay. Within a day I realized I wanted more colors. At first, I was intrigued by the variety of colors and all the shapes I could make. I continued to buy clay in different colors, purchased a few more tools and supplies, and forgot about sleeping for the next few weeks. I started researching the work of different artists, reading books on polymer clay, and making lots of beads. Making beads led the way to making pendants and pins, then earrings, and finally to fashioning colorful handles for all my tools. Then I thought, "Why not handles for serving pieces? Why not make magnets, knobs for drawers, key chains, and then actual chains made from the clay?" I found polymer clay to be very simple to work with, and it was increasingly clear to me that if I had a design idea, I probably could do it with polymer clay. This adventure began ten years ago, and I'm still excited about the creative possibilities of working with polymer clay.

If you are involved in crafts of any kind, you can apply the skills you've already learned to working with polymer clay. Polymer clay can be rolled, shaped, carved, painted, stamped, glued, layered, sanded, drilled, sewn, woven, crocheted, polished, even sent as a postcard. Can you begin to imagine how many different ways you might be able to use this amazing twentieth-century product to fulfill your creative ideas?

Over the last few years, I have been fortunate enough to meet and take classes with some of the best polymer artists in the country. In doing so, I have learned that there are as many techniques and ways of working with polymer clay as there are artists and craftspeople. Polymer clay does not have many rules, there are no rigid guidelines or absolutes, no right or wrong way. It's an amazing medium with incredible potential in everyone's hands. Polymer clay is easy and fun and can go anywhere your imagination wants to go.

—Kim

For me, polymer clay was love at first sight. I came across it more than ten years ago in a toy store, but I quickly realized that clay wasn't just for kids. In fact, I am constantly amazed by the beautiful works of art created by my fellow polymer clay artists.

My favorite thing about polymer clay is its versatility. It can be combined with so many different materials and used in so many ways that it's impossible to become bored. If you can imagine something, you can create it with polymer clay.

—Angela

Quick reference text

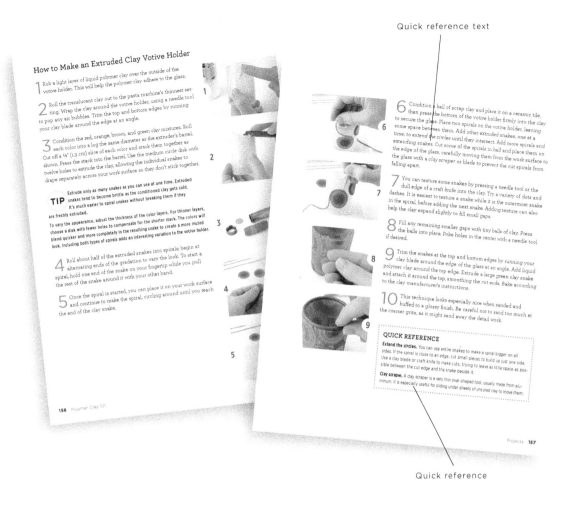

Quick reference

How to Use This Book

Each project in this book is designed to teach you a new technique or basic skill. This concept is outlined under What You'll Learn. A list of What You'll Need is provided for each project, beginning with the clay colors and proportions for mixing them, followed by tools and other materials. Throughout the projects, refer to the Quick References at the side of the page for definitions or elaborations on words printed in italics. Use this book as a resource for the explanation of different techniques and as a jumping off point for inspiration.

The online videos associated with this book are additional learning tools that will show you the essential techniques used for crafting with polymer clay. To access the videos, please visit www.creativepub.com/pages/polymer-clay-101.

History of Polymer Clay

Polymer clay has been in existence for over 70 years. It was developed in the 1930s in Germany by doll makers who wanted a strong, moldable clay for making doll heads and miniatures. The Fimo brand of polymer clay was further developed by Eberhard Faber who imported it to the United States in the 1970s. Cernit, another popular brand of clay, is made in Germany and imported to the United States.

Sculpey polymer clay was developed by Polyform Products Company for industrial use in the 1940s. However, it was not until the 1960s that the Sculpey clay was marketed as a sculptural medium for artists and craftspeople. In the mid-1980s, the Sculpey brand expanded the product line to a wide variety of different colors. In the 1990s, the Polyform Products Company developed the Premo! Sculpey brand of polymer clay, which had more elasticity and strength, making it popular with growing numbers of artists who wanted their clay to be more durable. Today, the Polyform Products Company has expanded the Sculpey line to include polymer clay for many different applications including Sculpey SuperFlex Bake & Bend, Sculpey Amazing Eraser Clay, Sculpey Ultralight, and Studio by Sculpey.

Kato Polyclay was developed in 2002 by Van Aken International and Donna Kato, a well-known polymer clay artist. Kato clay is designed to meet the needs of the serious polymer clay artist by providing strength, durability, and an excellent surface for polished finishes.

Composition

Polymer clay is manufactured by several different companies, each of which uses a slightly different formula. The difference in each company's formulas gives each clay unique properties both before and after curing. The only way to become familiar with the properties of each brand of clay is to experiment and learn about the differences. Polymer clay manufacturers change the ingredients and formula of a product periodically, either in response to changes in safety regulations or from a desire to enhance the features of the product. Some of these changes may affect how the product performs when you work with it and after it is cured. As you experiment, it's a good idea to keep a record, documenting which clay or combination of clays you used and how it worked in your project.

Safety

Polymer clay is made up of polyvinyl chloride, dyes, fillers, and a plasticizer that keeps the clay soft until it is cured. Polyvinyl chloride, also known as PVC, is the same plastic that is used in white plastic plumbing pipes. The clay has no water in it so it won't dry out. It has an indefinite shelf life if stored correctly and at the right temperature.

Polymer clay has undergone several studies to determine its safety and is labeled nontoxic based on the results of these studies. (See note opposite.) It is not meant to be used for or around food. If using a conventional oven, precautions should be taken to keep the clay and fumes contained. Small children should be carefully supervised when playing with polymer clay.

Note: There still remains some controversy over the acceptable levels of exposure to phthalate plasticizers in polymer clay. Studies done by Duke University Health System and Arts and Crafts Materials Institute in Boston have deemed polymer clay safe and actual transfer rates to skin and food to be lower than expected. Certain toxic phthalates were restricted in 2009 in the United States and the European Union. Most manufacturers have already changed their formulas to meet the new standards for safety.

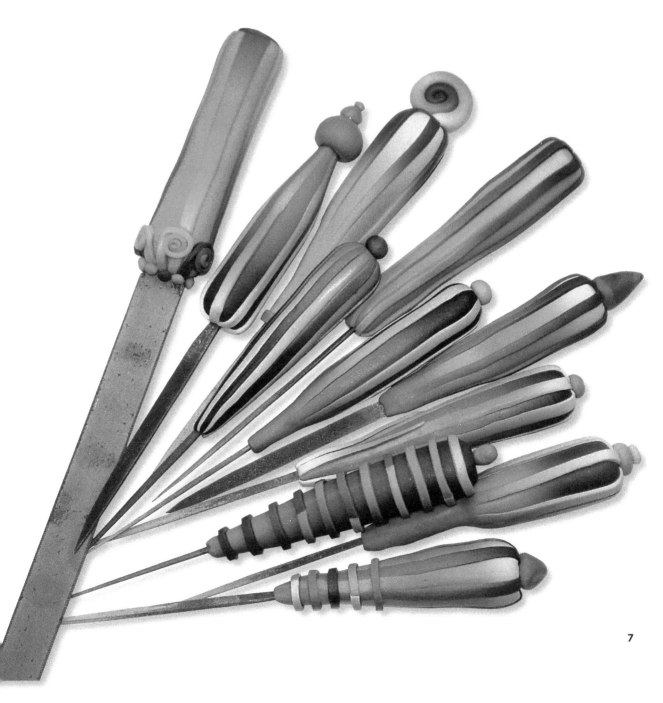

The Basics

Polymer clay is a very unique craft product. Once you begin to play with it and become familiar with the basic techniques for using it, many creative possibilities will emerge. Before you jump into making one of the projects in this book, though, take the time to read through this section carefully. Here you will find basic information about polymer clay—how to condition it, shape it, and cure it—and you will learn about the necessary tools and extra materials that you can incorporate as you gain experience with polymer clay.

Supplies and Tools

Crafting with polymer clay does not require a lot of tools and supplies, though there are some specialty products and tools that you may want to purchase as you explore all the possibilities of polymer clay. However, all you really need to get started are your hands, some polymer clay, and a few household items.

Clay Types

The availability of a wide variety of polymer clay brands offers great flexibility when designing projects. The polymer clays mentioned here are not the only clays available, but represent the most widely used clays. Each clay has specific characteristics, which means all clays are not equally suited for every project. As you work with the various brands of polymer clay, you will learn how to select

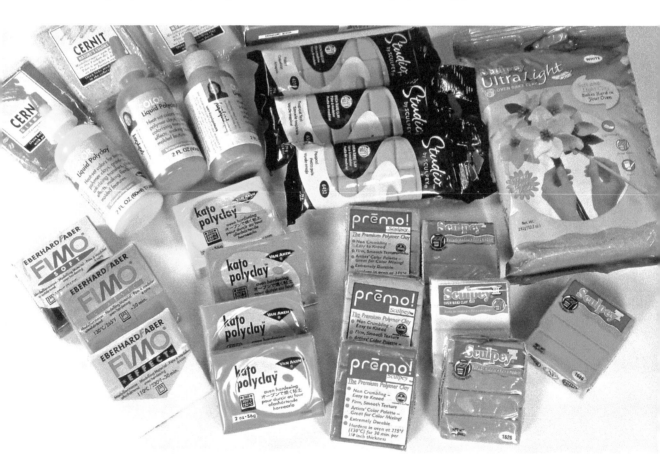

a brand for the characteristics most beneficial to your project. You will also see that different clays can be mixed together to join desirable properties.

Kato Polyclay. Kato is clay that can be used for most, if not all projects, because it is very strong, flexible, and holds details very well. The clay can develop a high shine when sanded and polished. It warms up slowly and therefore doesn't get sticky or overworked easily. Kato will take more time to condition (prepare for use) than some of the other clays, but the effort may be worth it for the finished properties. Using a food processor will help speed up conditioning.

Premo! Sculpey. This clay is easy to condition and comes in many colors. It remains flexible once cured and carves easily. It has a slightly shiny finish and polishes well. Premo! can be used for all kinds of projects.

Fimo Classic. This is a favorite clay for cane (see glossary) artists and anyone who likes the polymer to remain stiff enough to hold details well. Fimo Classic preserves the smallest details easily and responds slowly to warm hands. It is difficult to condition, and as a result, some clay artists use a food processor to speed up the process. It is very strong once cured.

Fimo Soft. This clay is much easier to condition than Fimo Classic. It is quite strong once cured, but because it is softer clay, it doesn't have the same detail-holding characteristics as Fimo Classic.

Original Sculpey. The first clay made by Polyform Products, this clay is easy to handle, economical, and comes in white and terra cotta. It should not be used for delicate designs because it becomes brittle once cured.

Super Sculpey. This product is mainly used by doll, mold, and model makers. It comes in a semi-translucent beige.

Sculpey III. This clay is easy to condition, comes in many colors, and has a nice matte finish once cured. It is not bendable after baking. Mixing in some translucent clay or combining it with other clays will help with its brittle characteristics. Sculpey III is not ideal for detailed cane work, because the clay is rather soft and can smear easily.

Studio by Sculpey. This clay comes in premixed designer colors, is easy to condition, and has a soft leathery feel to it. It is flexible once cured and has a matte finish.

Cernit. This clay has a new formula and comes in thirty-five colors. It is well regarded for its porcelain finish once cured. It is very strong and polishes well. It warms up quickly once conditioned.

Pardo Jewellery Clay. This clay includes beeswax as one of its ingredients and comes in a wide variety of metallic and jewel tones. It is very strong once cured.

Tools

Working with polymer clay does not require many tools. For the simpler projects, the only necessary tools are a pair of hands and a toaster oven. There are other tools—some you may have lying around your house and others that you can find in craft stores and elsewhere—that make it much easier to create hundreds of different projects from polymer clay.

A smooth work surface is essential. Many people find a large, thick piece of glass or plastic works well. Another good work surface is a 12" (30.5 cm) square tile of granite or marble, which has the additional benefit of staying cool in warmer weather.

TIP Place a cutting mat with a grid under the piece of glass. The grid surface of the cutting mat makes it very easy to cut straight lines and perfect squares when needed. You can use the grid to line the blade up as you cut the clay.

As with many other crafts, the workspace gets filled up quickly, so a bigger surface is easier and more enjoyable to work on than a smaller one. Index cards can be used as multiple small, movable

work surfaces on top of the glass or marble work surface. The additional benefit of using an index card when working on individual items is that the card is easily moved around and can be transferred directly into the oven for curing.

Never work directly on a finished piece of furniture. Polymer clay can leave marks and damage finishes on wood and fabric if left for long periods of time.

A roller is essential. Many people find a piece of 1" (2.5 cm) diameter PVC pipe works well and is inexpensive and easy to find. Acrylic rods are sold in craft stores for rolling clay; however, a straight-sided drinking glass works just fine too.

Clay will often need to be carefully cut into slices. Tissue blades are very thin long blades that are extremely sharp. They are the best way to cut precise slices of clay. To be on the safe side, cover the side that you hold with tape or paint it with nail polish so you don't pick up the sharp side by accident. Some people glue a craft stick lengthwise along top of the blade like a handle.

Index cards are great for transporting clay from the work surface to the oven. The clay will not stick to the paper and the paper won't leave a mark on the clay.

Although clay can be conditioned by hand, it can be quite time consuming and tiring to the wrists and hands. A pasta machine is a very useful piece of equipment. The rollers can be adjusted to make different thicknesses of clay sheets. The settings are numbered, starting with the thinnest setting at one. You'll find that making and mixing colors is quick and easy using a pasta machine. Culinary pasta machines can be quite expensive and once used for polymer clay should not be used for food. However, affordable craft pasta machines are now available for polymer clay artists.

An oven thermometer is necessary to determine an accurate temperature when curing the polymer clay. Some ovens can vary as much as 50°F (10°C) in actual temperature from the dial setting, which could mean clay is either not going to cure properly or may burn. A thermometer makes it easy to keep an eye on the temperature in the toaster or the oven.

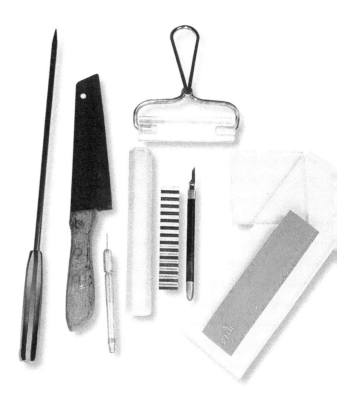

Additional Supplies

Investing in a few additional low-cost tools can provide even better results. Here are some of the tools and supplies you may want to acquire. Using a large, dull kitchen knife for slicing clay when first taken out of the package is easier and safer than using a tissue blade. A craft knife is very helpful for making small, delicate cuts in polymer clay. A brayer or acrylic roller is great for rolling out sections of clay and reducing canes. Once clay is cured, it is easy to drill. A ready-made hand drill works well or you can make your own drill by embedding a drill bit in a custom-made polymer handle (see "Skinner Blend Tool Covers" page 50). Knitting needles are used to smooth out ridges and places where edges meet. A polymer clay ruler, such as the Kato Marxit tool, is a great way to mark even segments for making beads. An acrylic rectangle is useful for rolling a clay snake and smoothing out fingerprints. A wavy blade can be used to make interesting cuts in clay. Not all clay projects need precise measurements, but a ruler will also enable a perfectly straight cut in a clay sheet.

Templates, Cutters, and Shaping Tools

Templates, cutters, and shaping tools are useful for creating a wide variety of shapes and design elements. Polymer clay can easily be cut into shapes with cookie cutters or with templates and a craft knife. Metal tubes cut in small sections can be used to make perfect clay circles of all sizes. Polymer clay also can be carved with linoleum cutters or wood-carving tools. Clay shapers, tools with little pieces of soft rubber at the end of a handle, are useful for smoothing out spots on soft clay.

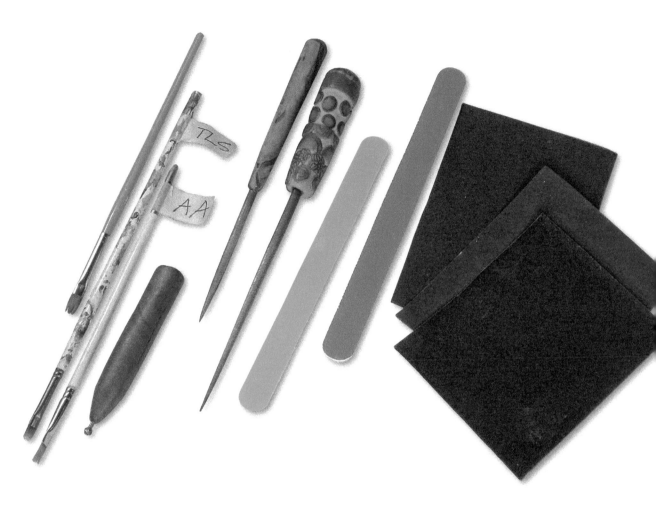

Metal files, foam nail files, and sandpaper are used to remove visible flaws and create a glossy finish on cured polymer. Polymer clay can be sanded and buffed to a beautiful shine. The dust created while sanding polymer should not be inhaled, so sand under water to keep the dust out of the air (and out of your lungs). Use wet/dry sandpaper or sponges in different grits to get the smoothest finish, starting from the coarser grits in sequential increments from 400 to 1200. Many people find that commercially available wet/dry foam nail files make sanding edges easy. Metal files can be used for hard to reach sections of cured clay. Any tip used in a Dremel rotary tool or a flex shaft can be converted to a hand tool by embedding the tip in a polymer handle. It is helpful to have a paintbrush dedicated for use with liquid polymer clay. Liquid polymer clay doesn't dry out, so the brush doesn't need to be cleaned every time it's used. Armor All protectant is often used as a release agent for molds and textures, and you may want to keep a separate brush for that use as well. Polymer clay can be painted before and after being cured. A few paintbrushes for oil and/or acrylic paint are good to have on hand.

(continued)

Molds and textures can be used to create surface effects. Most stamps, molds, and textures work well with polymer clay. Thin acrylic texture sheets and stamps without a backing can be rolled through the pasta machine with clay. Polymer clay can be pressed into molds and can be used to make molds as well.

Many products used in scrapbooking and other crafts can be used to add special effects to polymer clay. Polymer clays can be mixed with powders, pigments, glitters, inks, and foils. These materials can also be applied to the surface of the clay for a variety of effects and imitative techniques.

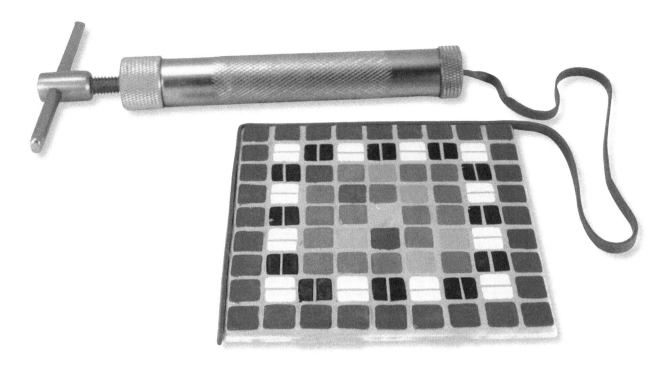

Oil or acrylic paints can be used to highlight or antique the surface of polymer clay. Both acrylic and oil paint work well with polymer. Clay can be painted before or after being cured. Paints can be applied after curing and partially wiped off for an antique look.

Several kinds of glues can be used with polymer clay. White glues can be used before curing the clay and in between layers of cured and fresh clay. Cyanoacrylate glue or E6000® should be used after curing to add pinbacks and ear studs.

A variety of effects can be created with the extruder tool. Weaving, knitting and crocheting, imitation chain maille, and basket making are a few techniques possible with an extruder.

Throughout this book a list of specific materials for the project will be given at the beginning of every chapter. The following items are not listed but should be included for each project:

- smooth work surface
- pasta machine
- toaster oven
- oven thermometer
- index cards

Techniques

Conditioning

All polymer clay needs to be conditioned. Some brands of clay will soften up without much effort, but all brands of polymer clay need to be worked to combine the ingredients when they first come out of a package. Polymer clay is soft and pliable when manufactured; however, once packaged and put on the shelf, it stiffens up and becomes too hard to shape easily by hand. By conditioning the clay, not only does it become easier to work with, but also its elasticity and strength return.

Once clay is conditioned, it will remain workable for a week or so, depending on the brand. The clay doesn't revert back to the same stiffness it had right out of the package, but it will need some conditioning to be softened again before using it.

How to Condition Clay by Hand

1 Start by slicing thin pieces from the block, using a dull kitchen knife.

2 On a smooth work surface, roll each piece into a snake. Roll the snakes together into a log.

3 Fold the clay over.

4 Twist the clay with one hand pushing away from you and one hand pulling toward you.

5 Continue rolling and twisting the clay log until it softens enough to form a flat sheet. Roll the hand-conditioned clay through the pasta machine on the thickest setting.

2

3

1

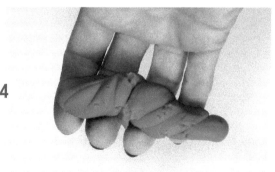

4

How to Condition Clay with a Pasta Machine

1 Start by slicing the clay into thin pieces as in step 1 for conditioning by hand. Set the pasta machine to the thickest setting. Roll each thinly cut slice through the pasta machine. One at a time, add a new slice to the slice just rolled and roll the two slices together through the pasta machine on the thickest setting.

2 When all the slices are combined roll the sheet through and fold over.

3 *Place the fold down,* and roll through the machine again.

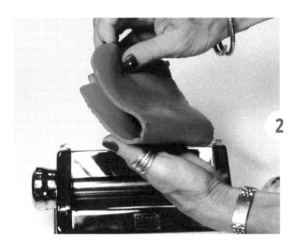

QUICK REFERENCE

Place the fold down. Always load the clay into the pasta machine with the folded side first to avoid creating air bubbles in the clay.

TIP If the clay becomes lopsided and a long rectangle is desired, use your hands to pull the clay while it's in the machine (shown below). Also, pull the areas with more clay toward the areas with less clay while rolling the sheet. This technique is very useful when making a Skinner blend or when a large uniform piece of clay is needed.

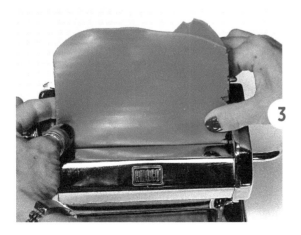

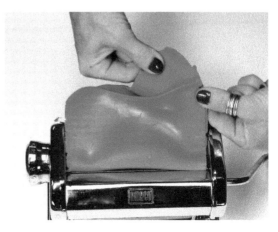

How to Condition Clay with a Food Processor

1 Start by cutting the clay into small squares. Stiffer clays often need to be chopped before rolling.

2 Process the clay in a food processor until little balls form. A small food processor both chops and warms the clay, making it easier to condition.

3 Dump out the clay.

4 Gather all the pieces together and compress the ground clay into a brick shape.

5 Cut the brick into slices. Pass the slices through the pasta machine one at a time, and then layer them together and run them through the pasta machine a few more times.

TIP If you like this method of conditioning, purchase a small, inexpensive food processor and use it only for polymer clay.

1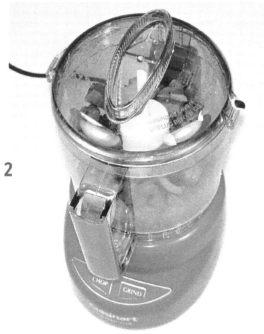

3

2

4

When conditioning the clay, many people find that some clay comes together faster than others. It can be well worth it to take the time to condition the clay thoroughly, because not only is the clay easier to use after conditioning, it is also stronger and has greater elasticity. If a particular clay continues to be hard to condition (crumbles, won't stick together) you may find that adding a small amount of translucent clay (any brand) will help. Adding translucent clay won't change the color of the clay unless a large portion is added.

TIP If the edges of the sheet remain cracked after rolling, continue by rolling out the clay until just combined, then step the pasta machine down to a smaller setting and roll the clay through again. The clay will soften up faster on a smaller setting. Bring the setting back to the largest setting when clay has softened and moves smoothly through the rollers. The thinner settings can create more air bubbles, so keep an eye on the clay when rolling.

Making new colors while conditioning clay is a great way to combine tasks. Whatever method you use to condition clay (by hand, pasta machine, or food processor) can also be used to mix custom colors. Slice the base colors needed to create the new colors and add them to each other while you condition.

There are a few easy remedies for clay that becomes too soft and sticky when conditioning. The easiest solution is to put the clay in the refrigerator for an hour or so. This is good practice when a warm day or warm hands make fingerprints hard to remove. Letting clay rest overnight is another way of making clay more firm.

Leaching can also be used to take some of the plasticizer (which makes the clay soft and pliable) out of the clay. To leach the clay, first roll out a sheet of clay. Place the rolled clay between two pieces of plain paper and place a book on top. Leave it for a few hours, or if the clay is still too soft, overnight. An oily stain on the paper will show where the plasticizer has leached out of the clay.

5

Storing the Clay

Once it has been taken from the package, polymer clay should be stored at room temperature, out of the sun, and covered in plastic wrap. Clay keeps indefinitely, but will harden with age, making it more difficult to condition and work with. The unused portions of the conditioned clay can be stored in plastic bags or wrapped in plastic wrap or wax paper. Keep separate, marked bags if using different kinds of clay. Although the different brands of clay can be mixed together, it's a good idea to know which brands are being combined. All the little pieces of clay left over from projects, known as scrap clay, can be used for bead cores and molds. Roll leftover pieces into separate balls of color. Store rolled-out clay between sheets of plastic wrap. Clay that is left touching will join together after a while, making it hard to separate colors that have been stacked together. Dust and pet hair will also adhere to clay left out for long periods of time.

Baking the Clay

Polymer clay requires heat to harden. Every brand has specific directions for the temperature setting and curing time listed on the package. The time required to cure the clay also depends on the

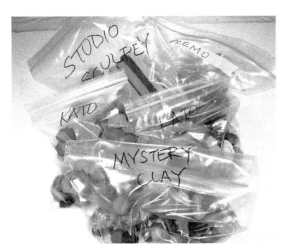

Labeling scrap clay when you finish each project will save you from working with "mystery clay."

thickness and size of the project. When cured at the right temperature, clay can be baked repeatedly without being harmed, making it possible to add design elements in several steps to a piece that has already been cured.

A toaster oven is the most common way to cure polymer clay, mainly because it is a good portable heat source for a relatively small investment. Once a toaster is used for curing polymer clay, it should be dedicated to clay use, removing the possibility of clay residue contaminating food. Polymer is nontoxic, but should not come in contact with food. When using a conventional oven to cure clay, keep the clay objects contained in a covered roasting pan lined with foil.

Baking clay directly on foil will leave a shiny spot on the clay. This can be eliminated by baking clay on index cards or parchment paper. A baking pan or ceramic tiles placed on the rack in the oven make an easy-to-access surface for loading polymer clay pieces on index cards or parchment paper into the oven. When making an unevenly shaped object that needs support in different areas, make a bowl out of foil and fill it with polyester fiber. Place the clay that is ready for curing in the fiberfill and cover loosely with more foil to bake.

Most toaster ovens will spike in temperature while heating up, so precautionary measures should be taken to prevent burning the clay. Tenting the clay with foil while curing will help the clay remain consistently at the correct temperature. Curing clay in a conventional oven is somewhat easier because of the larger size and more consistent heat, but a portable toaster oven offers the advantage that it can be moved to a convenient workspace and can be used only for clay.

The fumes from burned clay are noxious and should be avoided. When curing clay, always use an oven thermometer to check the temperature. Most clay starts to burn at a little over 300°F (145°C), so check the thermometer often until the oven reaches the required temperature. Kato clay

Use a polyester fiberfill blanket and tented foil to protect clay when baking.

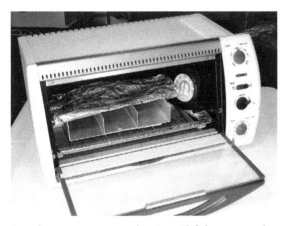

A good temperature gauge and tenting with foil can protect clay from burning.

is an exception here, and can be baked at 300°F (145°C). When mixed with other clays, Kato clay is fine being cured at 275°F (135°C). If the clay does burn, turn the oven off and keep the door closed. If the burned clay is in a toaster oven, unplug it and, if you can, carefully take the oven outside. If the clay burns in a conventional oven, keep the door closed and turn the oven vent on full and open the windows until the oven cools down. Then take the clay out of the oven and turn the oven back on for a half hour or so with the vent running to get rid of excess fumes.

Some burned clay can be sanded until the unwanted mark is gone. If the clay is melted and discolored, throw it away and start fresh. Always tent the pieces being cured with aluminum foil to avoid overcuring if the oven has a spike in temperature. Many ovens experience a spike in temperature when they are first turned on, in an attempt to quickly reach the correct temperature. If your oven does this, preheat and allow its temperature to stabilize before placing the clay in the oven.

If a large piece of clay is placed into an oven that's been preheated, the outside sometimes will cure faster than the inside and cause cracks to appear. If this happens, putting the cured piece in cold water when it comes out of the oven will shrink the size of the crack and often the crack will disappear. When working on a project or just planning to play with the clay, it's best to get the oven up to the right temperature and leave it running. Check the temperature every so often to make sure the oven is maintaining consistent heat.

Oven temperatures necessary for curing clay vary by brand. Always check the package instructions for the brand of clay you are using. A fairly common temperature setting is 275°F (135°C), although some experienced clay artists cure their clay at 285°F (140°C) for added strength. Be sure to tent light colors with aluminum foil to prevent them from darkening at higher temperatures.

The length of time for curing clay does not have to be very precise and should be adapted to the size of the piece. A piece of clay the size of a quarter and about ¼" (6 mm) thick should be cured for about 30 minutes. Larger amounts of clay will take longer to cure. Some projects will go back into the oven several times as new pieces of clay are added to the already cured one. As long as the temperature remains consistent, the clay should be fine for multiple curing times.

Mixing Colors

One of the best qualities of polymer clay is the color possibilities. Every color imaginable can be at your fingertips. Certain aspects of color and color mixing may require a little practice, but it is well worth the effort.

The primary colors are red, yellow, and blue. They are called primary colors because they cannot be mixed from other colors. In other words, if there is no red clay, red cannot be made from other colors and neither can the colors that red combines with, such as orange or purple. The secondary colors are the colors made by combining equal parts of two primary colors. For instance, red and yellow combine to make orange. Yellow and blue combine to make green, and blue and red combine to make purple. Combining the colors next to each other on the color wheel will make green/blue or orange/red. All the colors that we know are combinations of primary colors, secondary colors, black, and white.

Value is the light and dark of color. Adding black to a color will darken it and lower the color value. Adding white to a color will lighten it and raise the color value. Pure yellow, orange, and red are higher in value than blue, purple, and green. Blue, purple,

and green are considered cool colors and are used to make shadows. Yellow, orange, and red are warm colors and are used to make highlights. Describing a color is easiest when comparing it to another color or finding it on the color wheel. A cool yellow color is one that is closer to green and a warm yellow color is one that is closer to orange.

Keeping track of the colors you make with polymer clay is a very good way to get to know how to make new colors. Each color will have a formula—such as four parts yellow combined with one part black. Including the brand name will also help you to replicate the color. Red clay by Kato is not the same red as Premo!, and this holds true for all the other colors.

To start a color wheel, roll out each clay color to a medium setting on the pasta machine, place it on an index card, and cut out a small piece with a cookie cutter. Cut a small, circular hole close to the edge and bake the clay piece for 20 minutes at 275°F (135°C). When it cools, write the formula on the back with a permanent marker. Use abbreviations to keep it short. Some colors will have a lot of information on the back. For example: K, 2BLU,

Many custom colors of clay can be mixed from the three primary colors: red, blue, and yellow.

Blend the primary colors to create the secondary colors, expanding the range of colors available.

2BLK, 1W, 2Y indicates Kato clay, two parts blue, two parts black, one part white, and one part yellow. The numbers are approximate proportions, not strict measurements.

Many of the projects in this book feature a color recipe before the project to increase familiarity with the color wheel.

When conditioning clay and adding different colors together, it is possible to create a color that wasn't anticipated. Take a little piece of the surprise color and bake it. Write the approximate formula on the back and add it to the chips. Even if the new color doesn't appeal to you right now, it may be just the right shade at a later date. Put the chips on a ball chain or string to keep them organized.

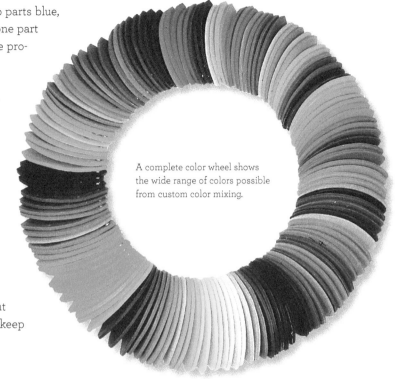

A complete color wheel shows the wide range of colors possible from custom color mixing.

Even more subtle color blends can be created by mixing primary and secondary colors.

Labeling color chips with the "color formula" makes it easy to replicate colors in future projects.

Shaping

Making shapes with polymer clay can be accomplished in a variety of ways. The simplest and most obvious way is to use your hands. There are many shapes that can be made between the palms of your hands. With a little practice, the shapes will become more consistent. While working with your hands is a lot of fun, it may be difficult to achieve the results desired with hands alone. With a little help from some simple tools, shaping polymer can be easier and the results more consistent.

Flat Shapes

1 Stack *playing cards* to the desired height of the clay. On a piece of paper or index card, place a conditioned ball of clay between the cards and flatten it with your hand. Roll the clay out between the cards.

2 Use cookie cutters, clay cutters (a), or plastic templates (b) to cut clay shapes from a sheet of clay.

A wide variety of bead shapes can be made from commercial bead rollers.

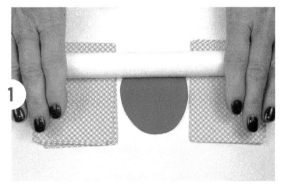

QUICK REFERENCE

Playing cards. A deck of playing cards provides a useful tool for maintaining an even thickness when rolling clay. Make two stacks with the same number of cards, and place the clay to be rolled between them. The stacks keep the roller level so the clay will be flattened to a consistent thickness. Remove the same number of cards from each stack to roll the clay thinner.

Balls and Beads

1

Roll a piece of clay between your hands. Keep the clay at the edges of your palms to make a more spherical form. To make a disk, flatten the ball either with your hands or with an acrylic square. To make an oval, first make a ball and then roll the ball up and down in the palm of your hand.

2

To make a bicone (two cone shapes pressed together at the wide end), first roll the clay into a ball. Place the ball on an index card and rest an acrylic square on top. Move the plastic in a circular motion while lightly pressing on the ball of clay. Keep rolling the clay until an edge appears around the ball and there is a pointed end on either side.

3

The shape of the bicone will vary based on how much pressure is used when shaping. The bicone shape makes great beads.

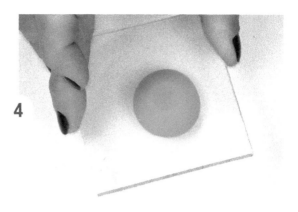

4

To make a lentil shape, make a bicone and flatten it with the acrylic square.

5

Lentil shape

TIP When making beads, let them rest overnight before making the holes. The clay won't distort as much as when you make the holes the next day.

Barrel and Tube Beads

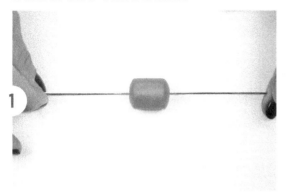

1

To make a barrel bead, first make a clay snake. Cut the snake into even segments and gently round the ends either with your hands or a piece of acrylic. To make tube beads, first make a large barrel bead. Pierce the bead with a 0000 knitting needle and move the barrel to the middle of the needle.

2

Gently roll the bead with the same action as when making a snake. Carefully pull the clay outward while rolling.

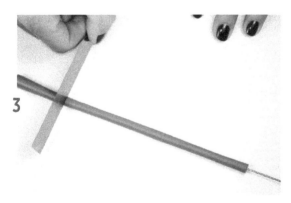

3

When the snake is the desired diameter, cut the ends off, leaving a small amount of the knitting needle showing. You can either cut the beads at this point and leave them on the needle for curing or cut them after they are cured.

Cabochons

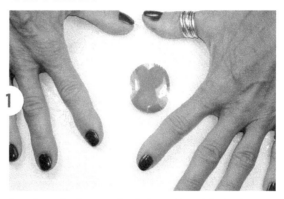

1

To make a cabochon, start by placing a piece of clay in the general shape of an oval template on an index card. Cover the shape with plastic wrap, holding it taut.

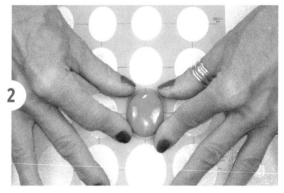

2

Press the template down on the clay and press firmly around the edges.

3

Remove the plastic wrap and use a tissue blade to cut around the edge. Place the plastic back on the clay and press down again with the template. Smooth the top of the clay with your finger.

Snakes

To make a snake of clay, gently roll the clay while pulling away from the center with both hands. Do not add much pressure to the clay; slide your hands outward while rolling very lightly. If your fingertips are angled toward each other, the snake will have fewer dents from your knuckles.

To make a striped snake, twist two snakes of clay together. Hold one end of the snake stationary with one hand and with the other hand roll the clay forward.

Reposition the snake with the moving hand and roll forward again.

Continue rolling until the two colors are smoothly joined but not blended.

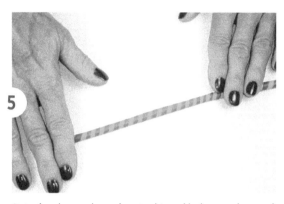

Striped snakes can be made quite thin and look great when used as borders and wrapped around beads. The swirl on the snake can be thinned and tightened by holding one end fixed while rotating the other end.

Mold Making

Polymer clay is a very practical material to use for making molds. There are many mold-making products that require mixing two different compounds. Most of these two-part mold-making products have a window of time when they are soft, and then they harden permanently. While the two-part compounds make great, bendable molds, polymer clay is a suitable choice for some projects.

In some situations, molds aren't required to be flexible, but being able to bend the mold makes it easier to release the clay being shaped. Sculpey Super Elasticlay and Sculpey SuperFlex Bake & Bend stay flexible after curing. Adding a small amount of Sculpey Super Elasticlay (Moldmaker) to any scrap clay will soften the clay and keep it bendable. Adding translucent clay to scrap clay also will make flexible clay that produces good, long-lasting molds.

Rubber stamps are used in many crafts. Stamps, intended for ink, make an impression where the raised picture on the stamp presses into the clay. To reverse the picture, make a mold of the stamp using this procedure.

How to Make a Mold

1 Roll out scrap clay on the thickest setting of the pasta machine. Cut the clay to fit the stamp with a ½" (1.3 cm) border all the way around the stamp. Stack three pieces of rolled clay together.

2 Roll the clay by hand to join the layers and roll out any *air bubbles* that may affect the structure of the final mold.

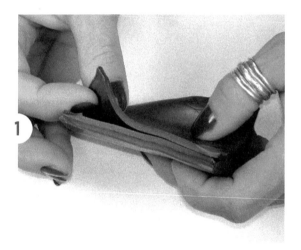

> ### QUICK REFERENCE
>
> **Air bubbles** can get trapped between layers and create holes in the clay stack. To prevent air bubbles when stacking layers, start at one edge and slowly roll each layer down onto the previous one. Compress all the layers together to eliminate any further bubbles.

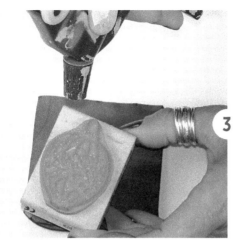

3 Spray the clay with water or Armor All protectant (found in the automotive section of hardware stores). This will act as a mold release agent to prevent sticking.

4 Place the clay on top of the stamp and press firmly and evenly.

5 Gently remove the clay from the mold. If the impression is incomplete or not deep enough, roll the clay out and repeat the steps. If all the desired detail of the image transferred to the mold, cure the clay for 30 minutes at 275°F (135°C).

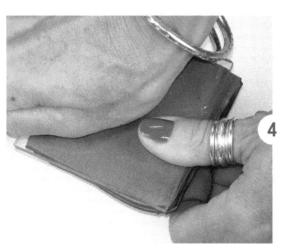

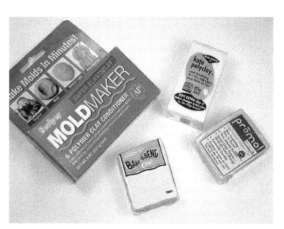

A variety of products are available for making molds.

Scrap clay is useful for making molds.

Sanding Cured Clay

Whether polymer clay is polished or not is a design choice. Some projects look better polished while others would lose character if they were shiny. Another option is to add texture to clay purposefully to keep fingerprints and nicks from showing. Pressing 180-grit sandpaper onto the clay is a simple way to add texture and hide small flaws.

A good way to approach working with polymer clay if you're after a smooth finish is: a) don't overcondition clay or use sticky clay, b) keep fingerprints to a minimum—try wearing tight-fitting latex gloves if prints are a problem, and c) smooth clay as much a possible before curing. It is much easier to smooth a piece of raw clay with a finger than to spend hours sanding dents and fingerprints off cured clay.

Sanding sponges come in several grits, often with different grits on either side. Wet/dry sand paper comes in a variety of grits, most of which can be found at your local hardware store. Grits starting at 100 and 180 are considered coarse, 220 and 320 are considered medium, and 400 and 600 fine. For a reflective, glasslike shine from polishing, 800-, 1000-, and 1200-grit sandpaper will be necessary.

If there are lots of scratches and fingerprints, start with 220 or maybe even 180. Sanding will remove layers of clay, so if the design is thin, make sure the design is not sanded away. Sanding must be done in successive order. If 220 is the first grit used, 320 is the next, then 400, 600, 800, and so on. If you can still see scratches at 400-grit, lower the grit to 180 and start again. If the cured clay is smooth, with few fingerprints and no nicks or dents, start with 400 or 600 and proceed sanding up to 1200. In order to get a high shine, sand in grit number order, starting with the lowest number needed for the particular piece being sanded.

Fill a pie plate with 1" (2.5 cm) of water. Dip the clay in the water or dip the sandpaper in the water

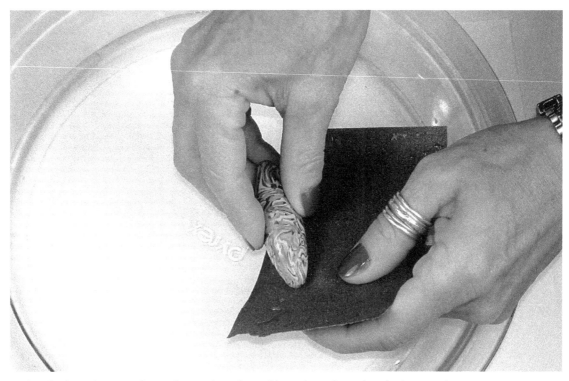

Sanding the clay under water reduces airborne polymer dust and keeps the sandpaper free of polymer residue.

to keep the dust out of the air. Sand the areas to be polished, which may be only an edge or it could be the entire piece. Flat objects are infinitely easier to sand than round. Placing a regular sponge on the bottom of the pie plate topped with sandpaper makes it easier to sand a curved surface.

Polishing

Once the sanding is completed, polishing is the next step. Polymer clay can be polished to a beautiful satin finish by rubbing the piece on a pair of jeans or a soft kitchen towel. A thorough sanding makes polishing a piece an easy step. To get a high shine, a very soft cotton or muslin head on a buffing wheel works well. A variable speed buffing wheel is ideal, but a regular one fitted with a clean head will work. To buff polymer clay, the piece must not be held stationary. Buffing wheels are powerful machines, and at high speeds, the friction will heat the clay and ruin the surface of the piece.

When polishing, stand facing the machine with both hands on the piece. Hold the clay piece at the bottom of the wheel. Don't press against the buffing wheel; just let the buffer lightly polish the clay. Move the piece back and forth just slightly to keep the clay from building up heat.

Jewelry-grade buffing wheels can be dangerous and should be approached with extreme caution. Always pull long sleeves back, tie up long hair, remove dangling jewelry, wear safety glasses, and pay careful attention when using the buffing machine.

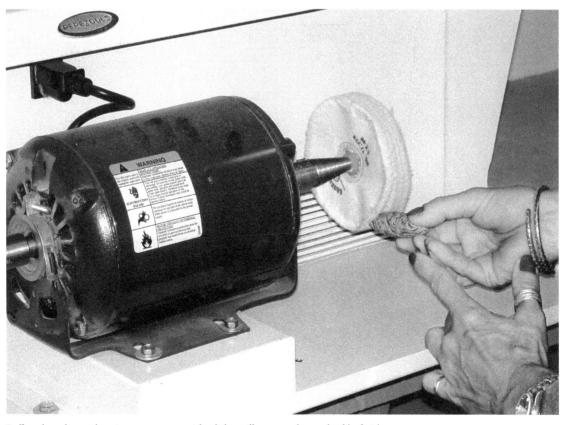

Buffing the polymer clay piece on a commercial polisher will create a glossy, glasslike finish.

Projects

Each of the projects in this section introduces you to new methods for using polymer clay. Some projects teach new ways to combine colors to create interesting effects or designs, like graduated color, marbling, or stripes. Many of the projects incorporate skills and materials that have transferred from other crafts, such as stamping, carving, image transfer, and metal leafing. Though some projects may take more time than others, they are not arranged by difficulty level, nor is it necessary to complete them in order. Choosing where to start might be a challenge. Be sure to read through all of the projects so you don't miss out on any of the fun!

Skinner Blend Bead Necklace

A Skinner blend is a graduated color shift across a sheet of clay. This technique was created by Judith Skinner and is widely used by polymer clay artists. Once the colors have been blended to form a gradual shift of colors, the clay can be used to make beads of graduated sizes to be strung into a necklace. The fascinating color shift makes a very chic piece of jewelry. Try the color combination here or use the color wheel (page 25) to help you design your own Skinner blend.

WHAT YOU'LL LEARN . . . .

- How to make a Skinner blend
- How to shape color-graduated round beads
- How to make disc beads
- How to make a toggle closure

WHAT YOU'LL NEED . . . .

KATO CLAY OR CLAY OF CHOICE

- olive clay mixture:

    2 oz (56 g) turquoise

    2 oz (56 g) gold

- mauve clay mixture:

    3 oz (85 g) purple

    1 oz (28 g) gold

- blue clay mixture:

    3 oz (85 g) blue

    1 oz (28 g) magenta

    pinch of gold

- ½ oz (14 g) magenta
- scrap clay

TOOLS

- acrylic rectangle
- tissue blade
- ruler

- craft knife
- awl or needle tool
- hand drill
- clay shaper
- round-nose pliers

OTHER MATERIALS

- thirty-two playing cards
- plastic wrap
- small piece of ½" (1.3 cm) tubing
- clear nail polish
- 1" (2.5 cm) 18-gauge wire
- 36" (0.92 m) nylon string, such as Conso or C-lon
- liquid polymer clay, such as Translucent Liquid Sculpey (TLS)
- size 6 seed beads in color to match clay

How to Make a Skinner Blend

1 Condition the clay colors using the listed formula to make three colors: olive, blue, and mauve. Roll each color out to the pasta machine's thickest setting. Cut triangles of each of the colors as shown in the photo.

2 Press the edges of the triangles together to make one *square sheet*. Notice that the triangles do not come to a point. If you use triangles that do not come to a point, the color will remain the same in the areas that are not touching other colors when folded over. Blending occurs where colors overlap.

3 Fold the clay end-to-end so that each color lines up. Where colors overlap, they will blend together. Where any color meets the same color, it will stay that color. You can get a good idea of what the blending will look like when you hold the clay as shown in the photo.

QUICK REFERENCE

Square sheet. A regular pasta machine is about 5½" (14 cm) wide, so make the sheet of clay the same width as the pasta machine rollers. It is easier to keep a Skinner blend square and uniform if the clay fills the width of the pasta machine.

Shift the color of the blend. If the color of a Skinner blend is too light, add a small snake of darker clay across the whole top of the blend. Conversely, to lighten the Skinner blend add a snake of lighter clay across the top of the sheet. Small pieces of clay can be inserted anywhere in the blend to make additional changes to the colors. Avoid mixing opposite colors unless you want to create muddy colors.

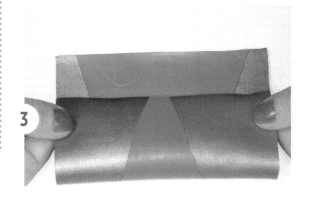

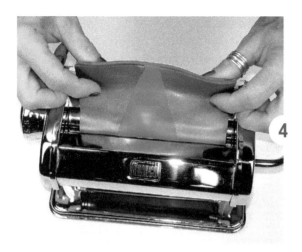

4 Set the pasta machine for the thickest setting. Place the clay into the pasta machine, folded edge first, and roll through. Fold the clay in half, matching the colors end-to-end and roll through the machine again.

TIP If the clay becomes uneven in the machine, pull gently away from the larger side toward the smaller side. Tugging at the clay to even it out before you roll can keep the blend uniform.

5 Continue to roll folded clay through the pasta machine until the colors start to blend and lose their distinct edges.

6 Another color can be added to the Skinner blend to *shift the color of the blend*. At this point in the mixing, the sample blend looked a little drab on the mauve side, so a small triangle of magenta clay was added on a diagonal.

7 Note how the magenta brightens the mauve color in the Skinner blend. When the clay is completely blended, roll the sheet out on the fifth-smallest setting on the pasta machine and cut the sheet into thirds.

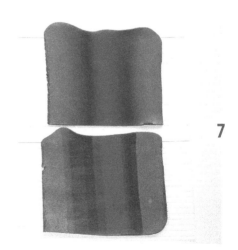

How to Make Round Beads

1 Roll some scrap clay into a snake to use as a base for the beads. Make the snake about ⅜" (1 cm) thick.

2 Use a ruler and tissue blade to cut one edge of the Skinner blend straight.

3 Place the scrap clay snake on top of the straight edge of the Skinner blend and roll the snake back and forth to adhere the edge of the clay to the snake.

4 Roll the snake over the Skinner blend, wrapping the snake with the sheet, until the first edge meets the rest of the sheet of clay. Lightly press the first edge onto the clay, leaving a mark.

5 Roll the clay back to reveal a line where the first edge met the sheet of clay. Cut along that line with the tissue blade.

6 Press the cut edges together and smooth them.

7 Continue rolling the covered snake using an acrylic rectangle until the snake is smooth and approximately ⅜" (1 cm) thick.

8 Line a ruler up to the edge of the snake and mark 1" (2.5 cm) sections using the tissue blade.

(continued)

TIP If the clay is warm and fingerprints are noticeable, use tight-fitting gloves or dust your hands with a small amount of corn starch.

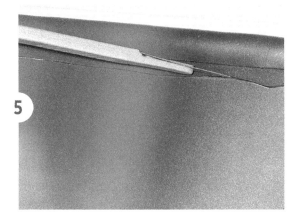

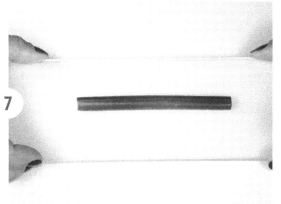

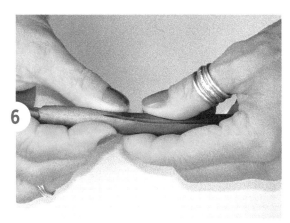

How to Make Round Beads *continued*

9 To cut through a snake without flattening it, roll the snake back and forth while gently pressing on the blade.

10 When the snake is used up, make a new one in the same way with a scrap-clay center. Continue the color blend by turning the snake around to keep the colors graduated. Cut at least six 1" (2.5 cm) pieces, six ¾" (1.9 cm) pieces, six ½" (1.3 cm) pieces, and six ¼" (6 mm) pieces. Also cut one 1½" (3.8 cm) piece for the center bead.

11 Pick up a ¼" (6 mm) section and carefully squeeze the ends closed while pulling the Skinner blend over the ends to cover the scrap clay center.

12 Carefully smooth the Skinner blend over the end of the bead.

13 Once the bead is covered in the outside color, roll it around in the palm of your hand to make it round.

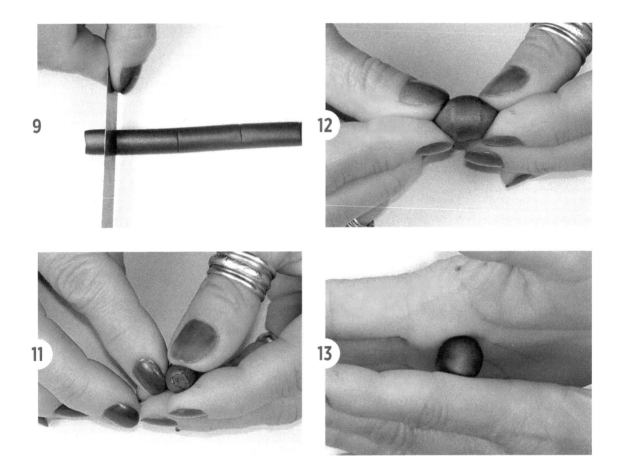

14 Repeat steps 11 to 13 for all the beads, keeping them in groups by size. Gently push a needle tool, awl, or large pin through each bead to create a hole. Hold the bead gently and push about halfway through with the pin.

15 Remove the pin and push it in from the other direction to meet the hole already started. This method keeps the hole smooth on both sides.

16 Fold an index card into accordion pleats to make grooves to hold the beads. The index card will not *leave a mark* on the sides of the beads.

17 Cure the beads for 25 to 30 minutes at 275° (135°C).

QUICK REFERENCE

Leave a mark. Curing round beads on a flat surface will leave a shiny, flat spot. A commercial bead tray is a great way to cure round beads, but index cards also work well..

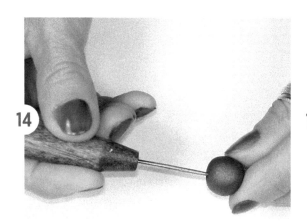

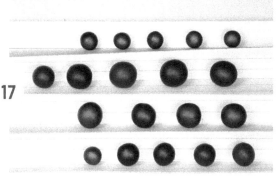

How to Make the Toggle

1 Cut two 1" (2.5 cm) pieces of the Skinner blend snake. Pinch ends of one of the pieces and make a round bead. On an index card, place the bead between two sets of sixteen playing cards and flatten with an acrylic square.

2 Tightly stretch plastic wrap over the flattened bead.

3 Press the metal tubing into the center of the clay over the plastic wrap to cut a hole.

4 Smooth the inside of the clay ring with your finger or a clay shaper. Roll out the second 1" (2.5 cm) piece of clay into a snake about the same diameter as the toggle ring.

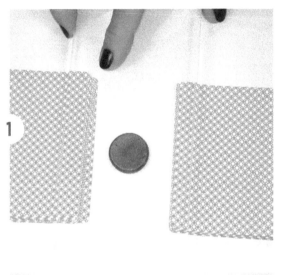

5 Place the snake on top of the toggle ring and measure ¼" (6 mm) past each side of the ring. Cut with a craft blade and smooth the ends.

6 Use a sharp blade to cut a slit in the snake about ⅛" (3 mm) long for inserting a wire loop.

7 Make the wire loop by placing the center of the 18-gauge wire on one side of the round-nose pliers. Bend the ends around to form a loop in the middle with ends facing opposite directions.

8 Put a drop of liquid polymer clay in the slit of the toggle bar.

9 Place the wire in the slit and top off with liquid polymer clay. Leave the loop in the wire showing and close up the clay slit with a clay shaper. Bake the toggle bar and ring on an index card for 25 minutes at 275°F (135°C).

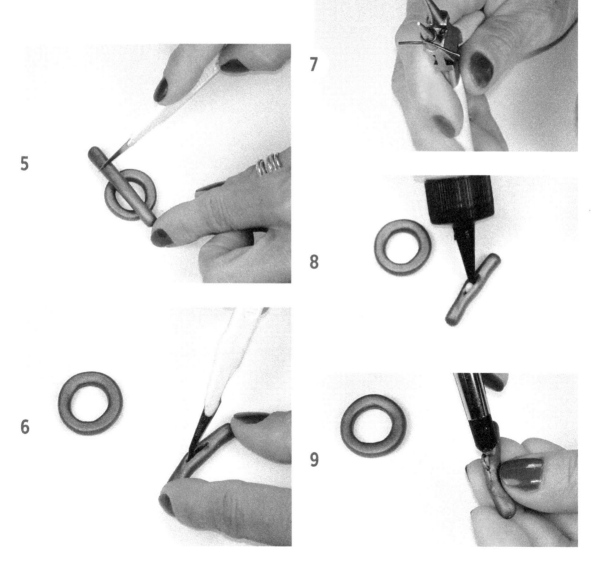

5

6

7

8

9

How to String the Beads

1 Line the polymer beads up by color order and size with the biggest in the middle and the smallest on the ends.

2 String the beads on nylon, alternating each polymer bead with a seed bead. Use a hand drill to make the hole in the last bead on each end a little bigger before stringing the bead.

3 Add enough seed beads at one end to reach around the clay toggle ring loosely.

4 With the nylon string, go back through the first seed bead and the last clay bead.

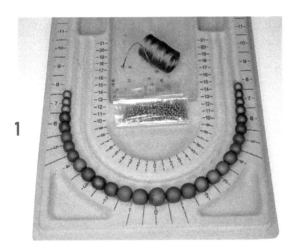

5 Tie a surgeon's knot below the last clay bead. (See glossary.)

6 Place the end of an awl into the loop of the knot and pull the knot down close to the necklace to make it tight.

7 String on five extra seed beads on the other end of the necklace and go through the wire loop on the toggle bar.

(continued)

How to String the Beads *continued*

8 With the end of the string, go back through all five seed beads and the last clay bead that has a hole that was drilled slightly larger.

9 Make a surgeon's knot in the nylon below the clay bead. Use the awl in the same manner as before to bring the knot down to the necklace.

10 Place a drop of clear nail polish on the knots to secure them and trim the ends of the nylon.

8

10

9

Variation

Make a polymer clay necklace with flattened beads for an entirely different look. Follow the same method for making the necklace with round beads. Before piercing the holes, flatten the beads uniformly, using the technique shown below.

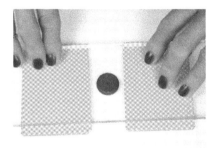

Line up two piles of playing cards, sixteen cards high. Place them on an index card. Put a bead between the piles of cards and press the bead down with an acrylic rectangle. The beads will be perfectly circular and will have very few fingerprints.

Then pierce the holes and cure the beads. A bead tray makes it easy to cure the beads in the oven without causing marks or flat spots. The advantage to flat beads instead of round beads is that they can cure lying flat if you don't have a bead tray.

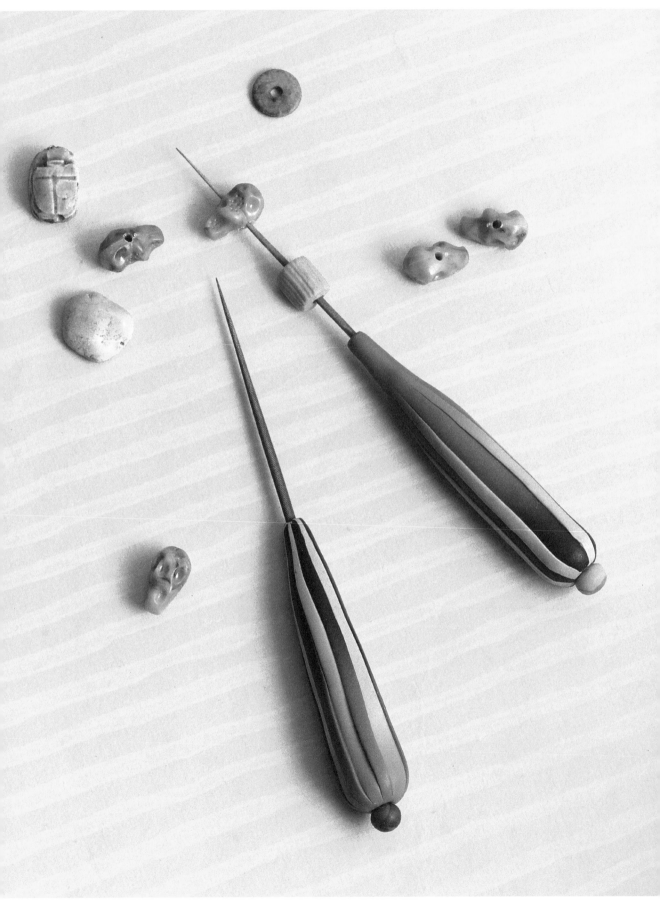

Skinner Blend Tool Covers

Skinner blends are useful for other projects besides jewelry, and once you learn the technique, you'll be inspired to use graduated colors for other projects. These tool handle covers not only spice up your craft space, they also make your tools feel more comfortable in your hand. The setup for this project is not exact and any number of combinations of colored triangles will give beautiful results. However, a significant color difference from the dark color to the light color in the Skinner blend will show off the stripes better.

WHAT YOU'LL LEARN...

- How to make a complex Skinner blend
- How to cover a tool
- How to add design elements to clay shapes

WHAT YOU'LL NEED..

CLAY

- 1 oz (28 g) black clay
- 1 oz (28 g) blue clay
- 1 oz (28 g) yellow clay
- light blue mixture:
    1 oz (28 g) white
    three pieces of blue
    one piece of black
    one piece of yellow

- green mixture:
    1 oz (28 g) yellow
    one piece of blue
    one small piece of black
- 1 oz (28 g) scrap clay

TOOLS

- half round file or any tool
- knitting needle
- tissue blade
- plastic roller
- clear plastic rectangle

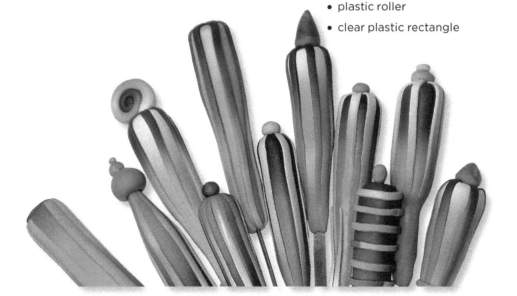

How to Make Skinner Blend Tool Covers

1 Condition the clays and mix the colors as listed. Lay out a Skinner blend as pictured using triangles of colored clays.

2 While rolling the Skinner blend through the pasta machine, place your finger on the rollers, lightly touching the edge of the clay about three-quarters of the way across the roller As you roll the clay out this will keep the clay to a specific width, about 4" (10 cm), and keep the edges neater. Roll the Skinner blend in the pasta machine to the fourth-thinnest setting.

3 Roll out a snake with the scrap clay to approximately ½" (1.3 cm) in diameter and 4" (10 cm) long. Put the Skinner blend on your work surface and cut a straight edge along one end of the clay using a tissue blade. Line up the scrap snake along the end of the Skinner blend.

4 Roll the snake over and press the cut edge of the snake against the blend on the work surface to make a mark.

5 Use a tissue blade to slice the clay at the mark.

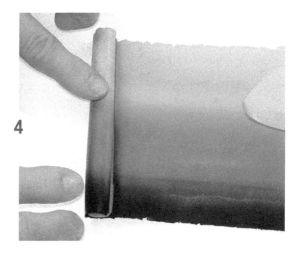

6 Line up the edges of the Skinner blend to enclose the scrap clay snake.

7 Roll a knitting needle over the seam to join and smooth the edges.

8 Roll the clay with a clear plastic rectangle to smooth the edges and even out the diameter of the snake.

(continued)

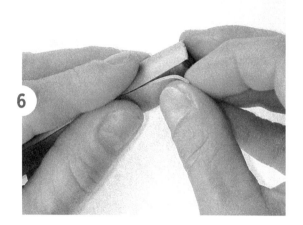
6

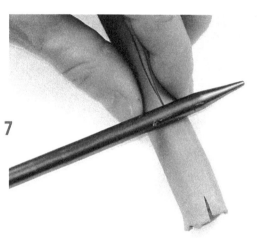
7

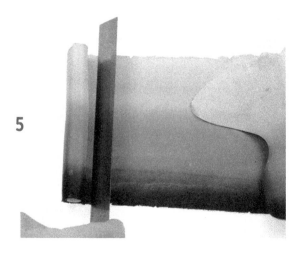
5

8

Skinner Blend Tool Covers *continued*

9 Cut the ends clean with a tissue blade.

10 Cut off the rough edges of the remaining Skinner blend sheet.

11 Cut six strips across the bottom of the Skinner blend approximately ⅛" (3 mm) wide.

12 Lay the strips one at a time along the clay snake.

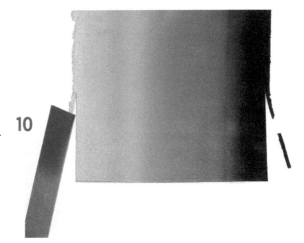

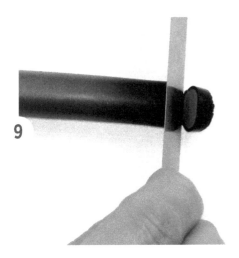

13 Place the strips in the opposite color direction from the blend on the snake. First lay one strip from one end to the other and press it down lightly. Hold the snake with the end facing you and place the second strip directly across from the first.

14

14 Fill in with the other strips evenly spaced along the snake, lightly pressing the clay to adhere it to the snake.

15 Cut the snake in two equal sections with a tissue blade.

16 Insert the end of a tool, such as a half-round file, into the clay snake at one end.

(continued)

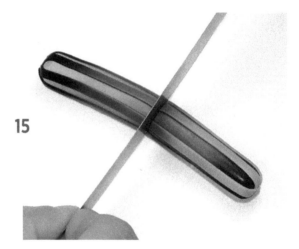

15

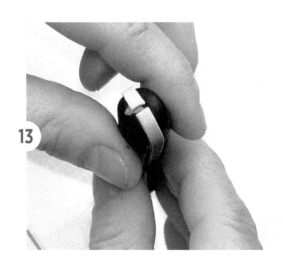

13

16

Skinner Blend Tool Covers continued

17 Gently pull the clay down the tool handle, using even pressure from all sides. Try to keep the stripes straight.

18 Dip your finger in water and smooth the clay slightly.

19 Use a blade to evenly trim the narrower end of the handle.

20 Insert a knitting needle into the wide end of the handle to form a depression.

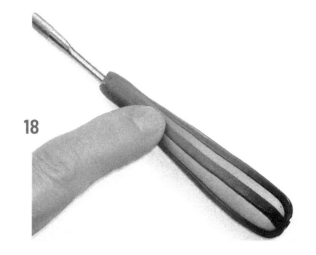

18

19

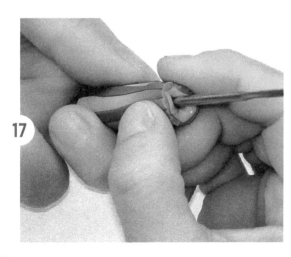

17

20

21 Roll a small ball of clay into an oval and press it into the depression in the handle.

22 Lay the handle on an index card and cure in an oven for 45 minutes.

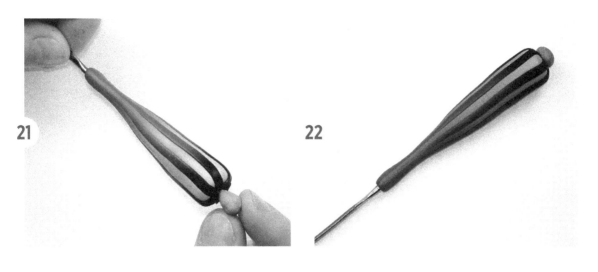

21

22

Variations

Make fancy handles for all your craft tools. Besides dressing up your craft area, the handles are very comfortable in your hand.

Marbled Clay Decorated Pen

Marbling is another fun technique for mixing clay colors. With this technique, the colors join together into a sheet of thin wavy stripes, but the colors still retain their own identities. Every combination of colors will make an interesting mix as long as the colors don't blend together too much. An ordinary pen becomes a classy writing tool with a new marbled clay cover. Once cured, the marbled look is further enhanced by sanding and polishing.

WHAT YOU'LL LEARN..............................

- How to make a decorative covering for an inexpensive pen

- How to combine colors to create the look of marble

WHAT YOU'LL NEED..............................

CLAY

- 1 oz (28 g) black clay
- burnt orange mixture:
    1 oz (28 g) yellow
    1 oz (28 g) orange
    one small piece blue
    one small piece purple
- yellow-green mixture:
    1 oz (28 g) yellow
    one small piece blue
    one small piece black
- ochre mixture:
    1 oz (28 g) yellow
    ½ oz (14 g) white
    ¼ oz (7 g) brown
    one very small piece black

- burgundy mixture:
    1 oz (28 g) red
    1 oz (28 g) purple

TOOLS

- tissue blade
- knitting needle
- roller

OTHER MATERIALS

- inexpensive round stick pen

How to Make Marbled Clay Decorated Pen

1 Condition clay and mix colors. Roll snakes approximately 7" (17.8 cm) long from each color of clay. If choosing different colors, use as many snakes of clay as desired, but try to keep a contrast between the colors. Cut some of the colors into two or three snakes for a more varied stripe.

(continued)

Marbled Clay Decorated Pen continued

2 Line all the snakes up together and roll with your hands to adhere them.

3 Roll the snake away from you with your right hand and pull the snake toward you with your left hand. The colors will begin to spiral.

4 Fold the snake in half.

5 Roll into a log. Continue to push forward with your right hand while pulling downward with your left to create a tighter spiral in the clay.

2

3

4

5

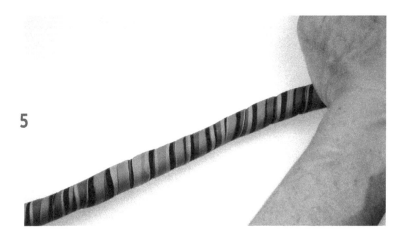

6 Once again, fold the snake over and roll it into a smooth log. Gently push the palms of your hands together while rolling the clay to form a log about 5" (12.7 cm) long. Slice the clay log lengthwise with a tissue blade, but don't cut all the way through to the work surface.

7 Open the two halves up and use a plastic roller to flatten the clay into a sheet.

8 Place the clay into the pasta machine with the stripes perpendicular to the rollers, and roll out on the thickest setting. Check the clay for air bubbles. Slice the bubbles with a tissue blade to let the air escape, but don't cut all the way through the sheet.

(continued)

6

7

8

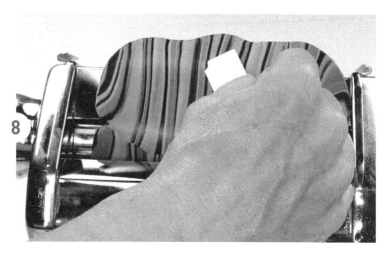

Marbled Clay Decorated Pen continued

9 Place the clay on your work surface with the stripes going horizontally. Using the tip of a knitting needle, score the clay in strokes perpendicular to the stripes in the clay. Don't press too hard, but do make a clear mark. Drag each strip in the opposite direction from the previous scoring. Completely cover the clay sheet with scoring marks perpendicular to the stripes.

10 Cut the sheet of clay to the size that will fit into the pasta machine. The clay must go through the pasta machine with the scored marks perpendicular to the rollers and the stripes parallel to the rollers. Roll the clay through the machine on the second-thickest setting, then roll on the third-thickest setting, and finally roll on the fourth-thickest setting.

11 Remove the ink cartridge from the plastic pen. Place the pen cover on a section of clay and use a tissue blade to cut the clay to fit the pen cover end-to-end. Cut a straight edge along the length of the pen.

12 Gently roll the clay around the pen cover to the other side of the pen. Cut the sheet of clay where you see the line from the first edge. Push the edges of clay together.

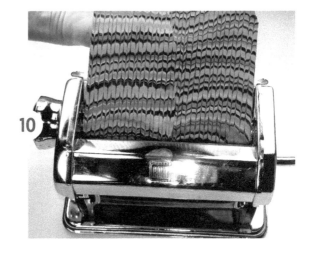

10

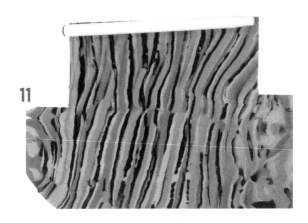

11

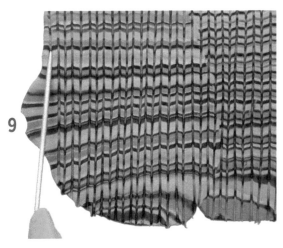

9

12

13 Use a knitting needle to smooth the seam.

14 Cut off the excess clay from the ends of the pen and smooth them.

15 Roll the pen with a plastic rectangle to remove fingerprints. Place the clay-covered pen on an index card and bake in the toaster oven for 30 minutes at 275°F (135°C). Sand and polish the pen cover after it has cooled from curing. Place the ink cartridge back in the pen cover after baking, and sand and polish the clay.

13

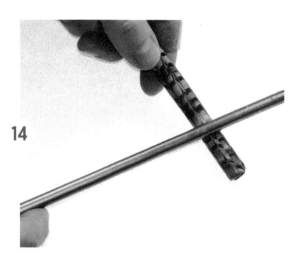

14

Variations

Sanded and polished pens

Bangle Bracelet from Simple Canes

Caning is an interesting, versatile technique that makes full use of the wonderful color properties of polymer clay. A cane is a log or snake of clay that has a colorful design running all the way through it. A slice made anywhere along the cane will reveal the same design. Thin slices from various canes were used to decorate the surfaces of these bangle bracelets. There are lots of ways to build canes, from simple jelly rolls to more intricate checkerboards, and this project will introduce you to many of them.

WHAT YOU'LL LEARN..

- How to make seven simple canes
- How to reduce a round cane and a rectangular cane
- How to enlarge a clay snake
- How to slice canes and apply them to a surface
- How to make a bangle bracelet, rings, and a pair of earrings

WHAT YOU'LL NEED..

CLAY

- Kato clay or polymer clay of your choice (except Sculpey III) in the following colors:
- turquoise mixture:
   1 oz (28 g) white
   1 oz (28 g) Kato turquoise
   ¼ oz (7 g) yellow
- light blue mixture:
   2 oz (56 g) white
   one pinch of black
   one small piece yellow
   one small piece blue

- gray mixture:
   1 oz (28 g) white
   one small piece black
- brown mixture:
   2 oz (56 g) brown
   ⅛ oz (4 g) black
- light brown mixture:
   1 oz (28 g) white
   ½ oz (14 g) brown
   one small piece black
- scrap clay

TOOLS

- acrylic rectangle
- tissue blade
- ruler or work surface with a grid
- knitting needle
- craft knife
- roller

OTHER MATERIALS

- cyanoacrylate glue
- empty soda can

How to Make a Bull's-eye Cane

1 Condition and roll the light blue clay out on the thickest setting of the pasta machine. Cut the clay into a 2" × 2" (5 × 5 cm) square with a tissue blade. Reserve the remaining clay. Roll the 2" (5 cm) square of clay tightly into a log.

1

(continued)

Bull's-eye Cane *continued*

2 With your hands angled toward each other, pressing from each end, roll the clay into a log about 2" (5 cm) long.

3 Roll a piece of light brown clay to the third-thickest setting on the pasta machine. Put the blue log on top of the brown sheet and cut the edges of the brown sheet along the length of the blue clay log.

4 Roll the brown sheet around the blue clay log until it touches the other side of the brown sheet. Use the mark left on the clay sheet as a guide and cut the second edge of the brown clay sheet. Pinch the edges of the brown clay sheet together.

5 Roll with a knitting needle to smooth the seam. Gently roll the log with your hands to adhere the two layers of clay.

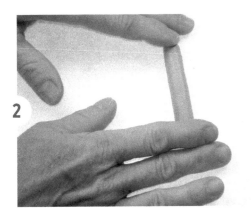

2

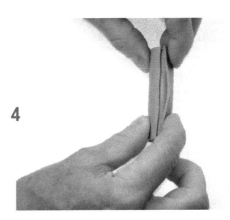

4

3

5

QUICK REFERENCE

Slice the ends off. Slicing the ends off a cane before reducing creates surface tension on the ends, which helps keep the clay from forming an inverted cone when rolled.

Middle of the log. Make sure the inside and the outside of the clay snake reduce at the same rate. By starting in the center when reducing the cane, the clay will move more evenly throughout the snake. Roll from the center out.

6 Roll the gray clay through the pasta machine on the fifth-thickest setting. Place the brown-covered blue log on the gray clay sheet using the same technique as in step 4. Cover the log with gray clay, trim the clay, pinch the ends, and smooth the seam. Note: When making a bull's-eye, any number of thicknesses and/or layers can be combined.

7 To reduce the diameter of the cane, first *slice the ends off*.

8 Place the edge of your hand in the middle of the log and gently roll back and forth to create a dent in the *middle of the log*.

9 Place your fingers in the middle of the log and roll, gently pulling outward.

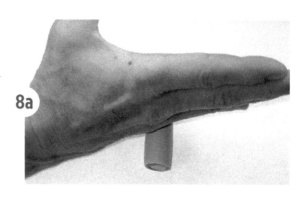

8a

8b

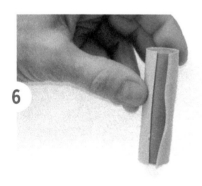

6

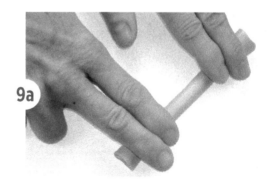

9a

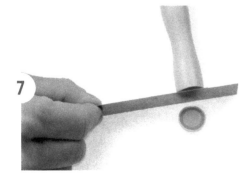

7

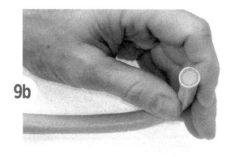

9b

How to Make a Jelly Roll Cane

1 Condition and roll the light brown clay to the fifth thickest setting of the pasta machine. Repeat with the brown clay. Cut the two sheets of clay into 1½" × 3" (3.8 × 7.6 cm) pieces. Place the pieces on top of each other and slightly flatten one end of the piece with a roller.

2 Cut the flattened edge straight with a tissue blade.

3 Carefully roll the clay into a log. Roll lightly with your hands to join the layers together, and cut the ends clean.

2

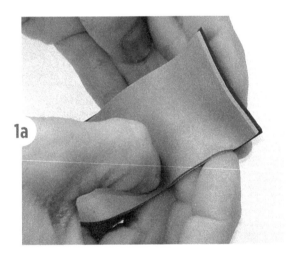

1a

1b

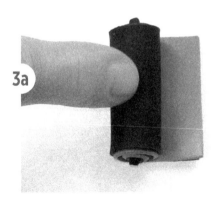

3a

3b

How to Make a Two-Color Striped Cane

1 Condition and roll the light blue clay to the fifth thickest setting on the pasta machine and repeat with the brown clay. Cut each color into four 1" × 2" (2.5 × 5 cm) sections.

2 Make the cane by alternating colors as you stack them.

3 Gently smooth each layer with your hand to remove air bubbles before placing the next layer.

4 Cut the rectangle in half and stack the two pieces together, making sure the stripes alternate. This will make a 1" × 1" (2.5 × 2.5 cm) stack of stripes.

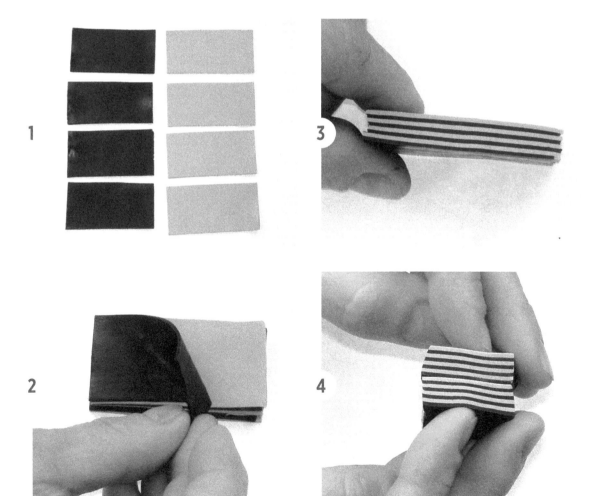

How to Make a Multicolor Striped Cane

1 Condition and roll the turquoise clay through the pasta machine on the third-thickest setting and cut two 2" × 1½" (5 × 3.8 cm) rectangles from the sheet. Change the setting to the fifth-thickest setting, roll the clay through the pasta machine again and cut two pieces of the same size rectangles.

2 Continue this procedure with each color. (The sample has a darker turquoise, as well, which is made by adding small-sized pieces of blue and black to the sample color.) Stack the colors in a random way, alternating darks and lights and thicker and thinner layers of clay.

3 Smooth each layer of color to remove air bubbles before adding the next layer. When finished with layering, cut the edges clean.

1

2

3

How to Make a Checkerboard Cane

1 Condition and roll the turquoise clay through the pasta machine on the thickest setting. Repeat with the brown clay. Cut three 1" × 2" (2.5 × 5 cm) pieces of each color of clay.

2 Stack them in alternating color layers.

3 Gently roll the layers together using a plastic roller.

4 Cut the layered stack in half (perpendicular to the layers), creating two 1" (2.5 cm) pieces. Set one striped cane aside. Cut the 1" (2.5 cm) striped cane in half (perpendicular to the layers) and then cut each half in thirds.

5 When assembling a checkerboard cane, the width of the stripe should be the same as the height, resulting in a square piece of clay. The striped cane, in this case, is six layers thick. When the stripe is cut into six even pieces in the opposite direction of the layers and placed together, alternating colors, each color becomes a square of the checkerboard.

6 Place one section against another, flipping the stripe so that a brown square is matched with a turquoise square. The next piece of clay should be flipped and stacked so that the brown square lines up with the turquoise square. Continue until all six layers are joined.

7 Turn the cube over and make sure the bottom squares are aligned correctly. Press the cube together to join the layers.

How to Make a Bull's-eye with a Striped Edge

1 Use the turquoise and brown striped cane reserved from the checkerboard cane. Press a piece of clear plastic down on the cane to reduce.

2 Slightly flatten each side. Notice that the insides of the stripe start to stick out from the edge and the pieces of clay on the outsides are smaller. While holding onto the striped cane, use your fingers to smooth and slightly pull the clay on the outside to the edge of the square.

3 Pull the clay and then flatten with the plastic roller to keep the layers even.

4 Trim the edges of the striped cane.

5 Cut the cane in half, lengthwise.

6 Stack the cut pieces together.

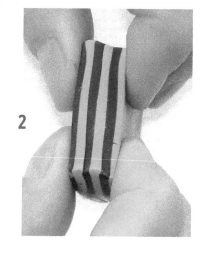

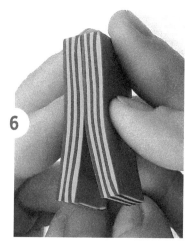

7 Cut the cane again and stack again.

8 Cut off a very thin section of the striped clay.

9 Gently roll the piece of striped clay to join layers and smooth out the piece.

10 Cut a 1" (2.5 cm) piece of the bull's-eye cane. Place the striped clay piece along the side of the bull's-eye cane and press to adhere.

11 Cut another slice of striped clay, trimming it to fit, and cover the outside of the cane. Roll to smooth the edges and join the clay together.

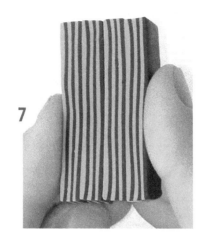

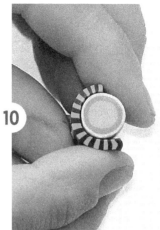

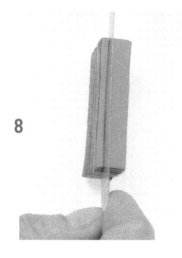

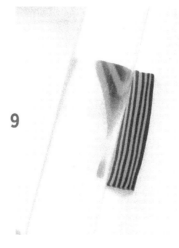

How to Make a Flower Cane

1 Condition and roll the turquoise clay through the pasta machine on the fifth thickest setting. Cover the plain bull's-eye cane with the turquoise clay.

2 Cut the sheet of turquoise clay to fit the bull's-eye cane and smooth the seam. Roll the turquoise-covered bull's-eye into a snake with a ¼" (6 mm) diameter. Cut the snake into five sections about 1" (2.5 cm) long each.

3 Shape each section into a teardrop shape for the petals.

4 Reduce the bull's-eye cane with the striped border to about ⅛" (3 mm) in diameter.

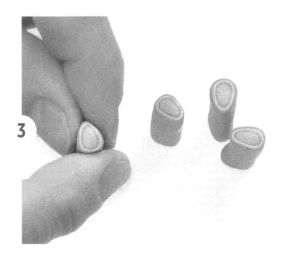

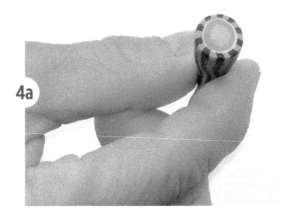

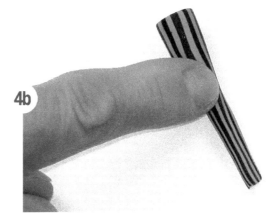

5 Cut a 1" (2.5 cm) piece of the stripe-covered bull's-eye cane for the center and stand the petals up around it.

5

6 Roll a piece of the gray clay into a short log, the same height as the flower petals, and a little bit smaller in diameter than the grouped petals.

7 Cut the gray log lengthwise into six pie-shaped sections (you'll have one piece extra).

(continued)

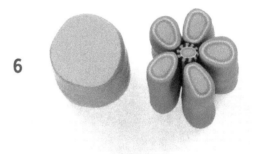

6

7

Flower Cane *continued*

8 Pinch the center of the gray sections to thin them out.

9 Fit the gray clay in between each petal section.

10 Turn the cane over and fit the gray clay into the same spots on the opposite side.

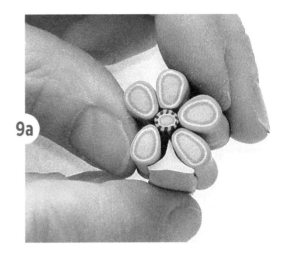

9a

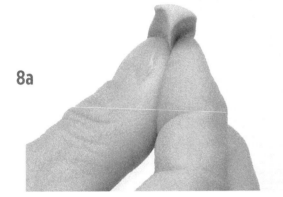

8a

9b

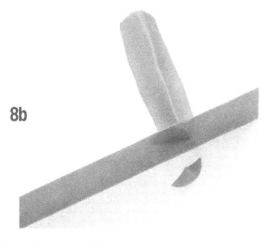

8b

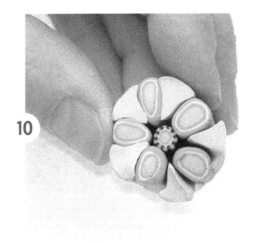

10

11 Trim the ends of the gray clay.

12 Cut off the ends of the cane.

13 Stand the cane up on the work surface and roll your hands back and forth while pressing in toward the cane.

14 This will reduce the cane slightly while keeping the ends flat.

12

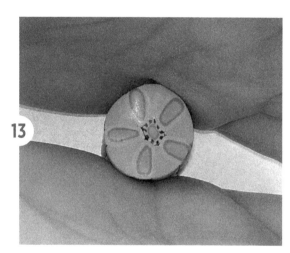

13

11

14

How to Make a Bangle Bracelet

1 Condition enough scrap clay to make a ⅜"
(1 cm) wide snake long enough to wrap around
a soda can. The bracelets can be made in any thickness; however, a bracelet thinner than ⁵⁄₁₆" (7.8 mm)
might break. Somewhere between ⅜" (1 cm) and ½"
(1.3 cm) diameter for the snake is a good place to
start. Wrap the snake around a soda can so that the
two ends overlap. Cut the snake with a tissue blade,
cutting through both sides at the same time.

2 Join the ends by twisting both sides back and
forth while applying pressure.

3 Place the snake back on the soda can to make
sure you have a good fit.

4 Try the "bracelet" on for size. If you need
more room to make the bracelet fit, add
another ¼" (6 mm) or so by pressing a new piece
of snake onto the end the same way the bracelet
was joined. Once you have determined the size of
the bracelet, make a note of the length for future
reference. The measurement for a soda can is a
little over 9" (23 cm).

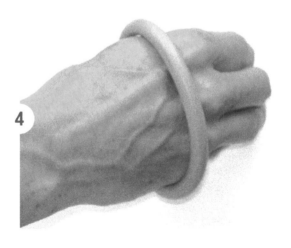

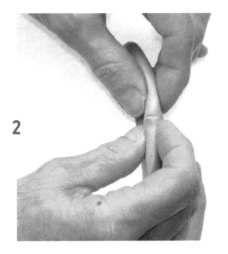

5 Cut the snake at the join and lay it on your work surface.

6 Use a plastic rectangle to even out the snake before adding the surface layers.

7 Slice very thin pieces of the canes and place them either in a pattern or randomly on the scrap clay snake.

(continued)

TIP Cutting canes into very thin slices takes a little practice, but is well worth the effort. Thicker slices will spread out when they are rolled and roll over thinner slices. The thinner the slices, the crisper the design will look when finished. Letting the canes rest overnight makes the clay stiffer and easier to cut thinly. The kind of clay that is used for the canes is also important. Kato clay and Fimo Classic are the stiffest clays and are great for making sharply defined canes.

5

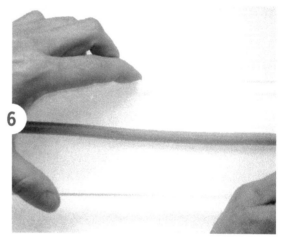

6

7

Bangle Bracelet continued

8 When the snake is completely covered, check for raised areas where the clay slice is thicker than the surrounding clay. Slice the higher areas off with a tissue blade. This technique will make the cane shorter and wider.

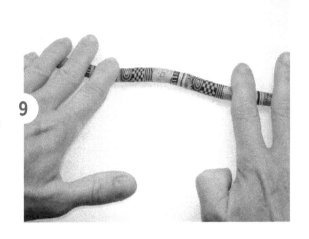

TIP Before rolling, check the work surface for stray bits of clay. Once the unwanted bits are rolled into the design, it can be very hard to remove them.

9 One way to combine all the cane slices together is to enlarge the diameter of the snake. Roll the snake gently with fingers spread out on either end of the clay.

10 While rolling, gently pull the clay ends toward the center of the snake. Make sure the ends enlarge at the same rate as the middle by placing a finger directly over the end of the snake while rolling and pushing toward the center.

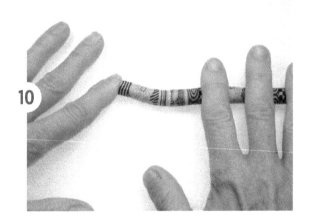

11 When the snake is about 6" long (15.2 cm), roll with a plastic rectangle to smooth out any uneven spots.

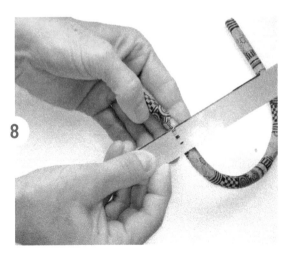

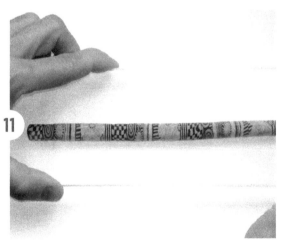

12 All the edges of the cut canes should be touching now and the clay design should be smooth. Roll the cane out and gently pull with one hand while smoothing with the other hand.

13 When the bracelet has reached the length required, wrap the clay into a circle the size of the bracelet and cut off the ends. If using a can, cut the ends on the can.

14 Attach the ends by scoring the insides of the snake with a tissue blade.

15 Put the ends together and press gently while twisting just a bit.

(continued)

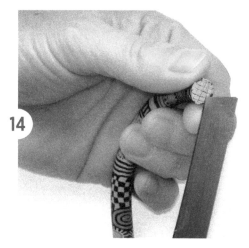

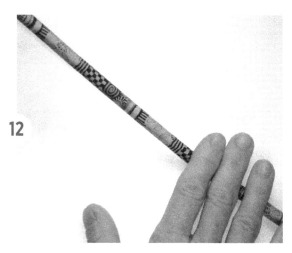

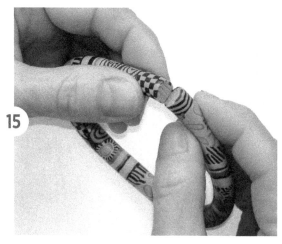

Bangle Bracelet continued

16 Roll back and forth with the bracelet on the work surface and your finger on the seam.

17 Don't press too hard or the snake will elongate and will have to be enlarged again. If the length becomes too long, just cut the snake at the seam and reroll to enlarge as shown in the previous steps.

18 Bake the bracelet right on the can. The small, half cans fit better in the toaster oven. If the size of the bracelet is smaller or larger than the can, lay it flat on an index card, formed into a circle. If using Kato clay, bake the bracelet at 300°F (149°C) degrees. For all other clays, follow the manufacturer's guidelines. If mixing different clays together, bake at 275°F (135°C) degrees for one hour.

19 The bracelets don't have to be sanded, but if a high shine is desired, sanding and buffing is a must. Start sanding the bracelet with 400-grit sand paper; sand with a wet/dry sanding sponge or paper and be sure to use water to keep the dust at a minimum. Be careful not to sand too much or the design will be sanded off. Proceed with 600- and then 800-grit sand paper. Buff on a buffing wheel or flex shaft with a very soft brush or muslin. If no power tools are available, rub the bracelet lightly on a piece of denim for a soft shine.

Variation

The example is completely covered with canes; however, a different and simpler bracelet can be made by covering the snake first with a background color. Roll the snake a bit smaller to start with and cover with the desired background color clay rolled out to the fifth- or sixth-thinnest setting on the pasta machine. Add the cane slices more sparingly to show off the background color.

16

18

How to Make a Bracelet with Rings

1 Follow Bangle Bracelet directions through step 19, making sure to make the bracelet about ⅜" (1 cm) wide.

2 When bracelet is cool, cut at the seam with a tissue blade.

3 Roll out two small snakes and twist them together as shown in the "Basics" section. Coil the clay snake around a ⁷⁄₁₆" (1.2 cm) dowel and bake for 20 minutes.

4 When the clay is cool, cut the rings off the dowel by cutting straight from one ring to the next.

5 Glue the rings together with cyanoacrylate glue.

6 Place the rings on the bracelet. Add silver rings, beaded rings, or any kind of rings.

7 Gouge a little of the cured clay from the center of the cut end of the bracelet with a craft knife. Glue the bracelet sides together with cyanoacrylate glue. Hold the ends together tightly for at least 20 seconds.

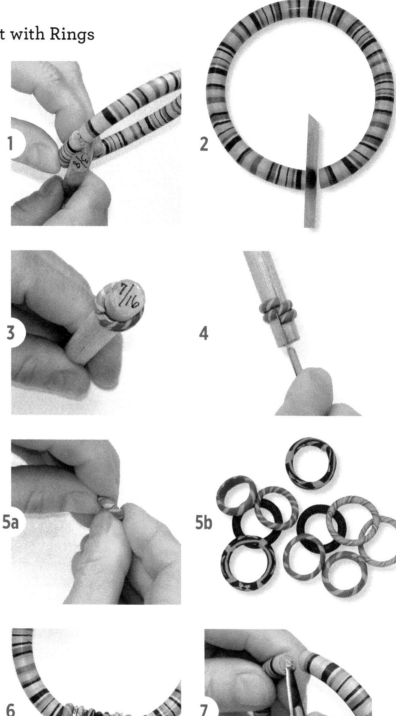

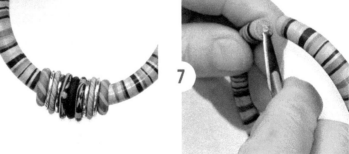

More Fun with Canes

Save your leftover canes. They are great form making small items like earrings or fancy beads, or for embellishing the surface of almost any polymer clay project. You never know when inspiration will strike.

How to Make Flower Earrings

1 Cover a small snake of scrap clay with the gray clay. Cut two 1" (2.5 cm) sections.

2 Pull the gray to cover the ends of the scrap clay and roll each piece into a ball. Flatten the balls slightly to make lentil-shaped beads. Cut two very thin pieces of the flower cane.

3 Place the cane slices on either side of the bead. Do the same for the other bead.

4 Use a knitting needle to smooth the edges of the cane. Bake on an index card for 25 minutes. When the beads are cool, sand and polish them. Use a hand drill fitted with a #67 or #68 bit which will match 20-gauge wire. Drill the bead at the top, making a hole at least ¼" (6 mm) deep.

5 Put a small drop of cyanoacrylate glue onto a wire with a wrapped loop and insert it into the hole. Hold it for 10 seconds.

6 Attach earring findings.

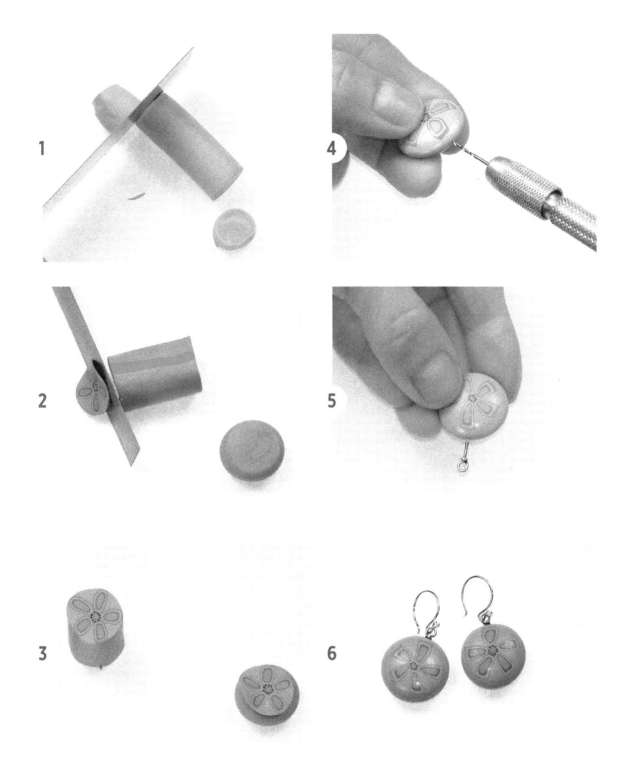

How to Make a Checkerboard Bead

1 Cut a cube of the turquoise clay to the same dimensions as the checkerboard cane (see page 71). Cut six very thin slices of the cane.

2 Attach the slices to the six sides of the cube, matching the checkerboard pattern as closely as possible.

3 Use a knitting needle to smooth the edges.

4 Pierce the bead and bake on a bead baking rack or on a bed of baking soda.

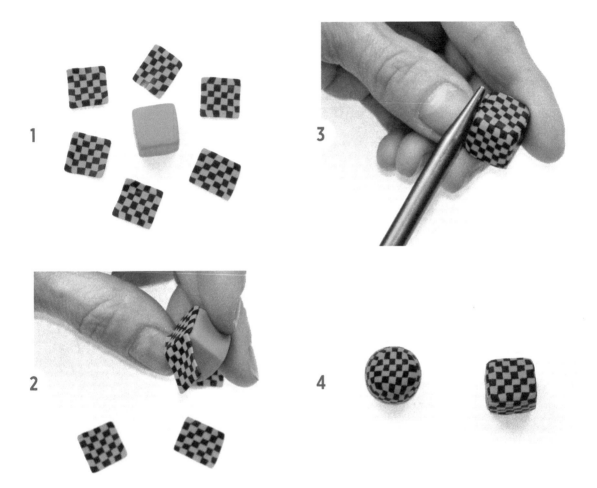

How to Make a Scrap Clay Cane

1 Make a pile of all the scraps from making the canes.

2 Roll out the pile with a roller.

3 Fold the clay in half and roll again.

4 Cut the clay in half and then in half again and stack the sheets. The scrap cane is a great way to utilize leftover clay from a large project. Slice the cane to cover items or use it as a backing for pins and pendants.

1

3

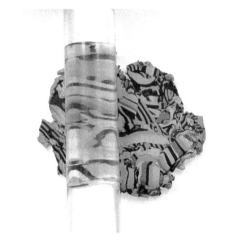

2

4

How to Make Striped Bead Earrings

1 Roll a piece of scrap clay into a snake and cover it with brown clay rolled out to a sixth-thinnest setting on the pasta machine. Cut a thin strip of the striped clay and place it on the snake.

2 Cut another piece of the stripe to cover the snake and cut the snake off where the stripe ends. Pull the striped clay toward the ends of the snake to cover the scrap. Press the ends towards each other to form an oval.

3 Make another bead.

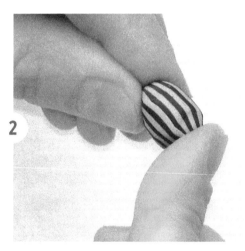

4   Pierce the beads with a head pin through the center.

5   Add caps to the beads and bake with the head pins and caps in place.

6   Attach ear wires.

4

5

6

Mica Shift Bowl

All the pearl clays have little specks of mica included in the clay. Mica naturally occurs in large, flat sheets, and the tiny pieces of mica used in the clay are also flat. When the clay is rolled the same direction several times, all the mica pieces lie in one direction, giving the top of the clay a bright shiny appearance. When you cut into the clay, you actually see the sides of the mica pieces, so the clay appears darker.

Techniques that take advantage of the mica's properties range from single-color canes to holographic effects created with deeply-textured rubber stamps. This project shows a simpler way to get familiar with mica shift, contrasting the shiny top of the bowl with the darker, polka-dots from the stacked cane's edges.

WHAT YOU'LL LEARN . . . .

- How to make and cure a hollow object
- How to attach raw clay to cured clay
- How to cut and fill holes with clay

WHAT YOU'LL NEED . . . .

CLAY

- blue pearl clay mixture

    3 oz (85 g) Kato pearl clay (or another brand of strong, stiff clay)

    1 oz (28 g) transparent clay

    ½ oz (14 g) Sculpey III blue pearl

    one small piece magenta

    ⅛ oz (4 g) yellow clay

TOOLS

- tissue blade
- paint brush

- craft knife
- plastic rectangle
- rubber clay shaper

OTHER MATERIALS

- Kato Clear Medium Liquid Polyclay
- polyester fiberfill
- masking tape for template
- metal tubing: ⅛" (3 mm) diameter, ½" (1.3 cm) diameter, ¾" (1.9 cm) diameter

Mica Shift Bowl

1 Put aside ½ oz (14 g) pearl and ¼ oz (7 g) Sculpey blue pearl clay. Then roll and condition the transparent clay with the pearl, the blue pearl, and the magenta clay. Roll clay through the pasta machine at least fifteen times, placing the folded edge of the clay into the machine first. If the shape of the clay becomes uneven, gently pull the clay when rolling to keep the clay approximately in a square.

2 Place the clay on your work surface and, using the outside edge of a roll of masking tape as a template, cut the clay in a circle.

3 With the remaining clay, cut and layer the pieces to make a stacked cane. Roll the cane with a roller to join the layers together.

4 Pinch the edges of the clay circle to thin the edges, like making a pie crust. Roll the edges lightly with a roller to smooth fingerprints.

2

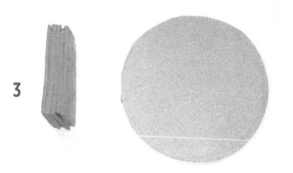

3

1

4

5 Fold the circle in half to make a crease.

6 Open up the circle and fold in half directly perpendicular to the first crease.

7 Open up the circle. The creases should cross in the center.

8 Use the tubing to cut circles out of the clay near the top edge of the bowl (rim). Save the scraps for another project. When cutting the circles, avoid the marks where the clay was folded. Do not cut circles in the very center of the clay bowl.

(continued)

TIP Use the flat end of a dowel to push out clay pieces from tubes.

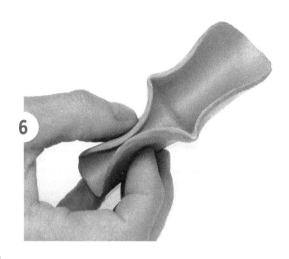

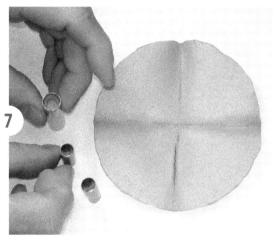

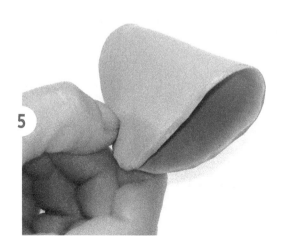

Mica Shift Bowl continued

9 With a tissue blade, cut a slice off the small cane of stacked clay. The cane slice should be slightly thicker than the clay surface in which you cut the holes. Cut circles from the cane and place them into the holes.

10 Place a piece of plastic wrap over the clay and use your fingers to smooth the whole surface. Roll the clay gently from the outside edge toward the center. Try not to distort the circle.

11 Drape the clay circle, centered on the end of the roller.

12 Use the marks made by folding the clay to indicate the center of the circle. Pinch the fold marks to make a ridge in the clay.

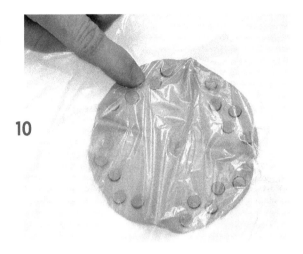

10

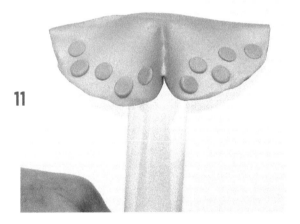

11

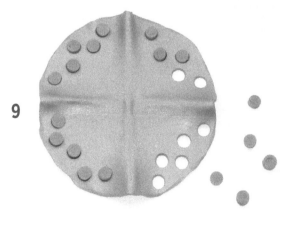

9

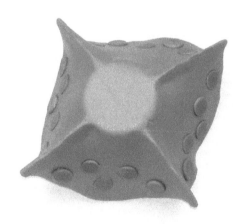

12

13 Take the bowl off the end of the roller, turn the bowl over, and shape it further with your fingers.

14 Put a small ball of polyester fiberfill into the bowl.

15 Turn the bowl upside down and place it on an index card. Put the bowl and index card in the toaster oven and tent it with foil.

16 Bake for one hour. Turn the oven off and wait about ten minutes. Carefully remove the bowl and bring it to a sink. Run cold water over the bowl to cool the clay. The bowl is fragile while it's warm, but can be cooled down quickly with cold water. Now is the time to sand any fingerprints or rough spots.

(continued)

TIP You can adjust the shape slightly while it's warm, holding it in place under the cold water. Too much bending will break the clay, so try not to depend on reshaping at the end.

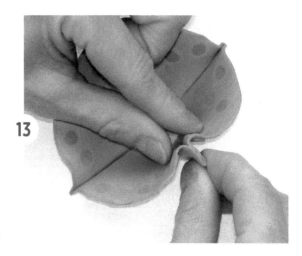

13

14

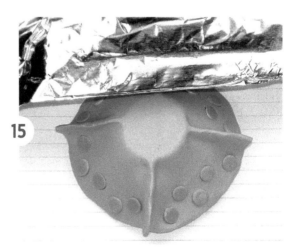

15

Mica Shift Bowl continued

17 Take the ¼ oz (7 g) of pearl clay and ⅛ oz (4 g) of blue pearl you set aside in step 1 and make a small Skinner blend sheet. Roll out the Skinner blend to the fifth-thickest setting on the pasta machine. Set aside.

18 To make the legs, roll out a snake of the cane clay and cut it into four ¾" (1.9 cm) lengths.

19 Form the shape of the legs by pinching one end.

TIP Using your finger to keep clay at a certain width can be very helpful while making small amounts of Skinner blends and longer pieces of clay. Hold a finger at the spot on the pasta machine that represents the desired width of the clay. Keep your finger there while rolling the clay.

17

18

19

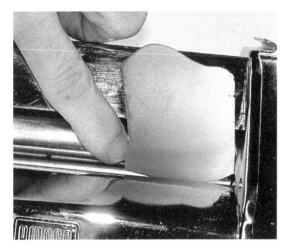

20 Cut small strips of the Skinner blend and place them on the legs, one strip at a time. Put four strips on one side of the leg, leaving one side without.

21 Cut a notch in the wider end of each leg with the tissue blade.

22 Place a small amount of liquid polymer clay into the notch on the leg. Press one leg onto each of the four folds at the bottom of the bowl and smooth the edges slightly.

(continued)

20

21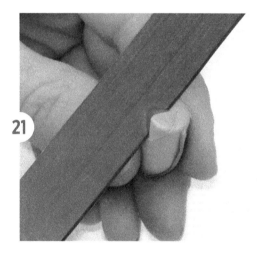

22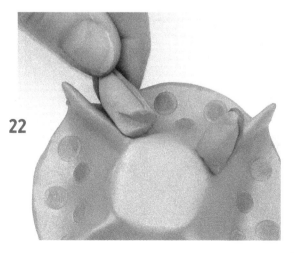

Mica Shift Bowl *continued*

23 Make sure all four legs are straight and the bowl stands evenly when you turn it over. Be careful with the legs while applying the leaves and flowers in the next step.

24 Mix a small amount of the blue clay mix with the yellow. Roll it through the pasta machine on the fourth-thickest setting. Cut small oval shapes with a craft knife for the leaves. Using the back of the craft knife, make a veinlike mark on the leaf surface.

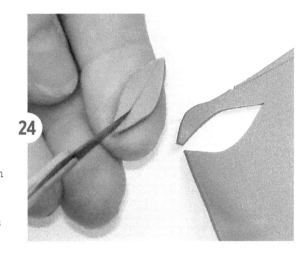

25 Use a paintbrush to apply small amounts of liquid polymer clay to the four corner folds on the rim of the bowl. Cut four ¾" (1.9 cm) circles and four ½" (1.3 cm) circles from the Skinner blend.

26 Place the smaller circle on top of the larger one.

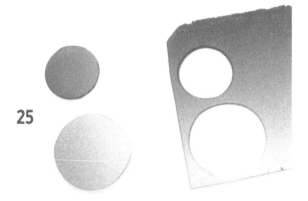

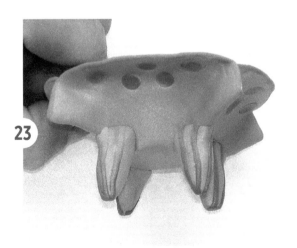

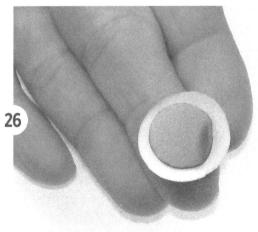

27 Press the pointed rubber clay shaper into the middle.

28 Pull the edges of the circles away from each other to look like flower petals. Put a leaf on the folded edge of the bowl and then place a flower.

29 Use the clay shaper to press the center of the flower into the fold. After all the flowers and leaves are placed, bake the bowl at 275°F (135°C) for 30 minutes, standing up in the oven on its legs and tented with foil.

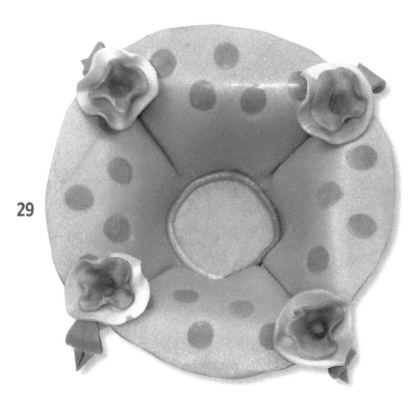

Painted Striped Beads

Though polymer clay comes in lots of glorious colors, you can also paint it with acrylic paint to add stripes or other designs. To make the beads for this necklace, the paint is applied to the clay before it is cured. After baking, the paint is permanent.

WHAT YOU'LL LEARN...

- How to paint with raw clay
- How to form caps on beads
- How to make a different toggle

WHAT YOU'LL NEED...

CLAY

- navy clay mixture:
    - 2 oz (56 g) blue clay
    - 1 oz (28 g) black clay
    - 2 oz (56 g) purple clay
- one small piece magenta
- blue clay mixture:
    - 2 oz (56 g) navy clay
    - ½ oz (14 g) yellow clay
- 1 oz (28 g) white clay
- ½ oz (14 g) blue clay

- green clay mixture:
    - 1 oz (28 g) yellow clay
    - one piece black clay

TOOLS

- plastic or polymer clay ruler
- tissue blade
- Poly-Tools bead tray and pins or 0000 knitting needle and folded index card
- small paintbrush
- ½" (1.3 cm) circle cutter

- ⅓" (8.5 mm) circle cutter
- ¼" (6 mm) circle cutter or circle template and craft knife
- hand drill with a #67 drill bit

OTHER MATERIALS

- cyanoacrylate glue
- 4' (12 m) nylon thread in coordinating color
- five small chain links
- one large jump ring
- green acrylic paint

How to Make Painted Striped Beads

1 Condition and roll the navy clay into a snake about ¾" (1.9 cm) in diameter. Make the snake about 15" (38 cm) long. Use the Marxit tool or a ruler to mark the snake every ½" (1.3 cm). For an 18" (45.7 cm) necklace, you'll need twelve beads.

1

(continued)

Painted Striped Beads continued

2 Cut the snake with a blade at the marks and roll each bead into a round. Pierce the beads with a 0000 knitting needle or use the pins in the bead baking rack. Cut four beads in half to make eight smaller beads. (These beads won't have a blue cap, just a stripe and a green end cap.)

3 With a small, flat paintbrush, paint five to seven stripes on each bead while holding the bead on a pin. If the paint is thin, wait until the first coat is dry and then paint a second coat. Let the paint dry.

4 Roll out the blue clay to a medium thickness, and place it on your work surface. Paint all over the clay, but leave some of the clay color showing through. Let the paint dry.

5 Cut circles in the blue clay for the caps to the beads. Use a ½" (1.3 cm) circle cutter or a circle template and a craft knife. Cut twenty caps.

TIP Acrylic paint is water-based, so if you make a mistake just run the bead under water before the paint dries and start over.

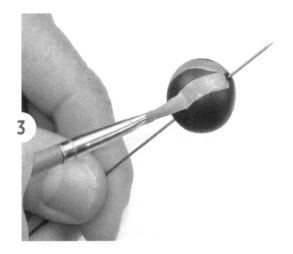

3

4

2

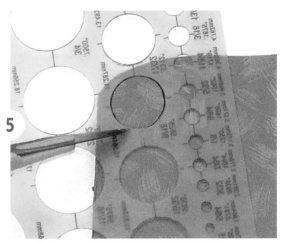

5

6 Make a hole in the circles at the center mark.

7 Place the clay circles on the pin on either side of the bead and gently press them into place.

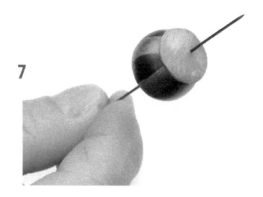

7

8 Roll out the green clay to a medium thickness, and use the ⅛" (3 mm) cutter to punch out circles. Place a green circle on the caps on either side of the bead and press to join the clay together. Also, the eight smaller beads need a green mini cap.

9 Make thirteen mini lentil beads. Cut twenty-six circles in the blue painted clay with the ⅓" (8.5 mm) circle cutter. Put two circles together with the painted side facing out and press the edges all the way around.

(continued)

8

TIP Pieces of brass tubing work well for cutting circles in clay. Small cookie cutters also do the trick.

6

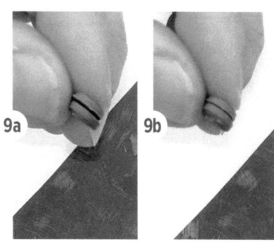

9a   9b

Painted Striped Beads continued

10 Pierce eleven of these lentil beads through the center, like a doughnut, and pierce two through the length of the bead.

11 To make the clasp, make a toggle bar and ring with the blue clay sheet. Wrap the painted clay around a very small snake, about ⅛" (3 mm) in diameter and 3" to 4" (7.6 to 10.2 cm) long. Join the edges of the wrap, and roll with a plastic rectangle to smooth the seam.

12 Cut the toggle bar about 1⅛" (3 cm) long—it does not have to be exact. Shape the snake into a circle and cut across both sides with a tissue blade. The diameter of the ring should be a little more than half of the length of the bar.

13 Join the ends of the ring.

11

12

10

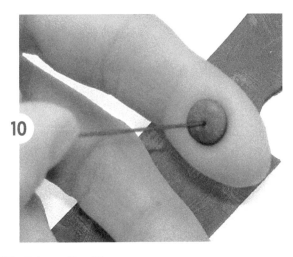

13

14 Cut the jump ring in half and bend the pieces into a U shape.

15 Roll four tiny balls of green clay and place them on the bar and the ring. Put the chain on a U and press it into the bar part of the clasp. Press the other U into the ring.

15

16 Place all the beads and the clasp on the bead tray and cure in the oven for 30 minutes at 275°F (135°C). The beads will not be sanded because of the paint. Acrylic paint should be applied before the clay has been cured so it becomes permanent. To string the beads with nylon thread, paint some cyanoacrylate glue on the last 3" (7.6 cm) of the thread and wait at least one hour for the glue to dry. Drill the hole a little bigger on the four small striped beads.

17 Use the drill to enlarge the lengthwise hole in the two lentil beads.

(continued) **16**

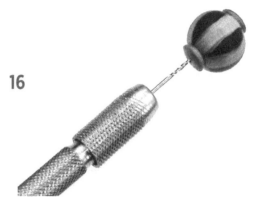

14

17

Painted Striped Beads continued

18 String two small striped beads, the lentil, and one end of the clasp onto the thread. Pull the beads to the end of the thread, leaving about 6" (15.2 cm).

19 Bring the tail of thread back through the lentil and make a knot around the core thread.

20 Pull the tail through the first striped bead and make another knot.

21 Bring the tail thread through the next striped bead and make a knot with the core thread. Cut the short tail end and continue adding beads and knotting until the end. At the end, string the two striped beads, the lentil, and the clasp, and go through the same process as above to finish.

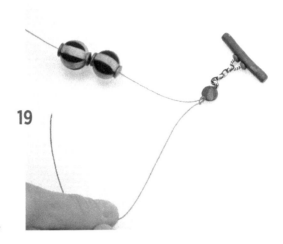

19

20

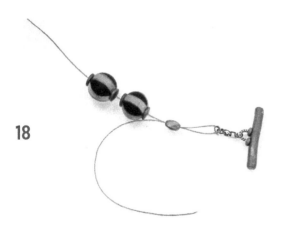

18

21

Variation 1

1 Condition and roll the navy clay out and taper the edges on either end. Use the polymer clay ruler to mark the graduated clay.

2 By using a graduated snake, the beads will also be graduated.

3 To find the correct size for a cap, hold the circle template over the bead to see which size is the right cap. If the necklace is graduated beads, the caps will have to change with the size of the bead. The circle template makes finding the right-sized cap easy.

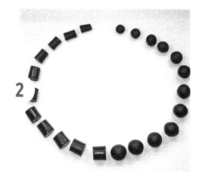

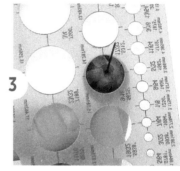

Variation 2

The colors on this necklace are purple, black, and burnt orange. The design made on the caps is from a stamp. The paint was put on the stamp with a sponge and then stamped onto the clay instead of painted with a brush. Also, the beads are all the same size and the small beads are real stones.

Antiqued Spoon and Fork Serving Pieces

Ordinary serving utensils are transformed into one-of-a-kind pieces when you add textured polymer clay handles. For this project, acrylic paint is applied after the clay has been cured. The paint collects in the depressions of the clay's texture to give the handles an antique look.

WHAT YOU'LL LEARN . . . .

- How to make a large patterned mold
- How to use Sculpey UltraLight clay
- How to create an antique effect using paint

WHAT YOU'LL NEED . . . .

CLAY

- scrap clay
- Sculpey Superflex or Super Elasticlay
- green clay mixture:

    2 oz (56 g) translucent clay

    tiny pinch of black, green, and yellow
- one-quarter of a package Sculpey UltraLight clay

TOOLS

- plastic roller
- paintbrush

OTHER MATERIALS

- Kato Clear Medium Liquid Polyclay
- white glue
- deeply patterned large bead or button
- large spoon and fork
- sponge with scouring pad
- acrylic paint in green and brown
- baking soda
- foil

How to Make Antiqued Serving Pieces

1 Roll out some scrap clay and add a small amount of Sculpey Superflex. Stack up four layers of clay and roll to join the clay together.

2 Press the patterned bead into the mold several times to form an all-over pattern. Bake the clay at 275°F (135°C) for 25 minutes.

(continued)

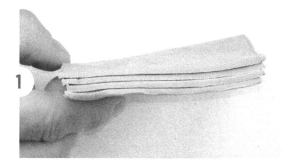

Antiqued Serving Pieces continued

3 Use the scouring portion of the sponge to rough up the ends of the serving pieces. Paint white glue on the ends and let them dry.

4 Roll out the Sculpey UltraLight clay with the roller (the pasta machine is not as effective with the UltraLight clay). Roll it to about the same thickness as the thickest setting on the machine. Place the utensils on the clay and cut out the shape twice.

5 Place the clay on either side of the utensil and pinch the sides.

4a

4b

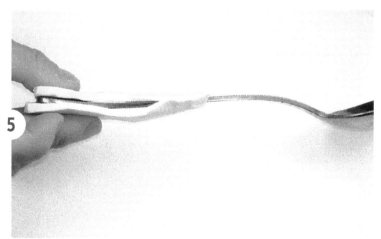

5

6 Smooth out the clay and bake at 275°F (135°C) for twenty minutes. Paint the cured UltraLight clay with white glue and let it dry.

7 Roll out the green clay to the third-thickest setting on the pasta machine. Lay the green clay sheet on the mold created in step 1 and press lightly to transfer the impression to the clay sheet.

8 Lay the serving utensil on the green clay and trim the clay to fit one side of the utensil.

(continued)

6

7

8

Antiqued Serving Pieces *continued*

9 Smooth the edges, almost smearing the edge around the sides of the utensil.

10 Bake for twenty minutes at 275°F (135°C) in a foil dish filled with baking soda.

11 When the clay is cool, paint a small amount of liquid polymer clay on the edge of the patterned cured clay.

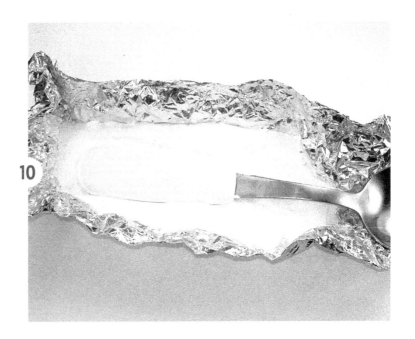

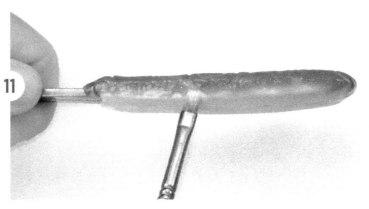

12 Repeat the process in step 7, using the uncured green clay and the mold, making sure to cover the edges. Bake the clay for another twenty minutes.

13 Sand the utensils if desired. Mix a small amount of green, white, and brown acrylic paint together. Brush on the paint, getting the paint into all the areas of the design.

14 With a damp paper towel, rub the high areas of paint off, leaving the paint in the deeper areas of design to create an antique look.

15 Let the paint dry completely. Sand and polish if a high shine is desired.

15

Stamped Key Chain

Rubber stamps are useful tools for creating designs in polymer clay, sometimes in ways that might surprise you. For this intriguing key chain, the swirly pattern of a rubber stamp is transferred to the clay surface by first making an impression and them trimming away the background. You'll be amazed at the results, and once you learn the technique, you'll soon imagine all kinds of ideas for using rubber stamps.

WHAT YOU'LL LEARN. . . . .

- How to transfer the raised design from a rubber stamp to clay
- How to use liquid polymer clay
- How to make a striped edge from a cane

WHAT YOU'LL NEED. . . . .

CLAY

- Skinner blend from Kato yellow to magenta
- a small amount of white and black added to the blend
- ½ oz (14 g) each of black and magenta
- coordinating colors for stripes
- ⅛ oz (4 g) black clay

TOOLS

- tissue blade
- paintbrush
- roller
- small tube cutter

OTHER MATERIALS

- plastic wrap
- Kato Clear Medium Liquid Polyclay
- design stamp
- 12-mm soldered ring

How to Make a Stamped Key Chain

1 Make a Skinner blend using a triangle of yellow and a triangle of magenta. Add a very small strip of white and black across the colors to subdue the yellow and pink. Roll out the blend on the third setting of the pasta machine.

(continued)

1

Stamped Key Chain continued

2 Roll out black clay on the thinnest setting of the pasta machine. Place the black clay on the Skinner blend. Start in one corner and press the black down on the Skinner blend. Try to join the clays together with no air bubbles.

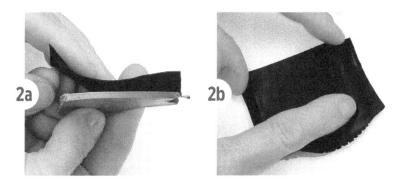

3 Dribble a few drops of water on the black clay and spread it all over the clay.

4 Using a stamp with a deep design, place the wet clay onto the stamp.

3

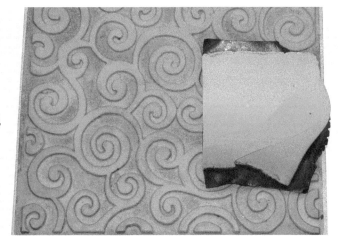

4

5 Cover the clay with plastic wrap.

6 Press the clay into the stamp with your fingers, making sure that all of the clay is pushed into the design. Press firmly but not hard enough to rip through the clay. Gently pull the clay off the stamp and check the design impression. The impression on the clay should be very deep and even.

7 Drape the clay on a plastic roller. The roller is a good surface for this step because the clay will not slip on the roller, and the curved surface of the roller makes it easier to trim in between the high points on the clay.

(continued)

5

6

7

Stamped Key Chain continued

8 Use a tissue blade to slice the high areas from the sheet of clay, being careful not to cut too deeply.

9 When the entire design has been exposed, remove the clay from the roller.

10 Put the clay on your work surface and place a piece of plastic wrap on top. Gently smooth the clay with your fingers or with a roller.

11 Cut the clay into two even rectangles. The shape does not need to be exact at this point.

12 Paint a small amount of liquid polymer clay onto the back of one of the pieces.

13 Place the pieces together, pressing gently to remove air bubbles.

14 Use a tube cutter to make a hole through the clay at the top of the shape.

(continued)

11

13

12
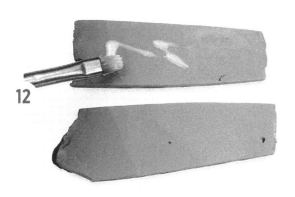

14

Stamped Key Chain continued

15 Use a tissue blade to refine the shape.

16 Make a small slit from the hole to the side of the piece. Insert a large soldered ring into the hole.

17 Paint a small amount of liquid polymer clay at the cut and reconnect the clay.

18 Bake the clay in a bed of baking soda. Stand the ring up in the baking soda and make sure that the piece of clay lies flat for curing.

19 Make a striped cane with black and magenta clay. Roll each color out on the third setting of the pasta machine and stack the colors (see page 69).

15 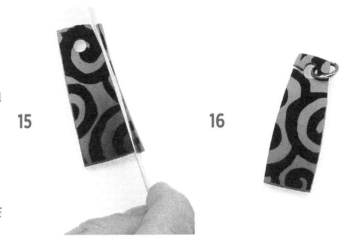 **16**

17

19

20 When the clay is cool, paint a small amount of liquid polymer clay onto the edges of the piece. Cut thin strips of the stripe to cover the outside edges. Lay the strips in place on the edges and then gently press to join.

21 Use a tissue blade to cut the excess striped clay from the front and the back.

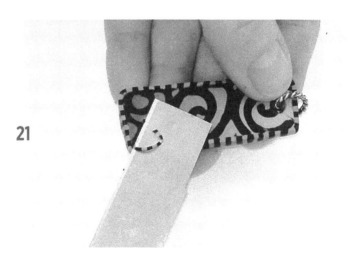

22 Bake the clay again for 25 minutes at 275°F (135°C). Sand and buff the clay when it is cool. Attach the soldered ring to a key chain ring.

Stamped Journal Cover

Journaling has become wildly popular, and the quest for unique journals is never ending. The covers for this journal are made from sheets of polymer clay that have been accented with stamped designs using acrylic paint. You can change the look with different colors and stamps, so every journal you make is a singular work of art. What a great gift!

WHAT YOU'LL LEARN . . . .

- How to make polymer clay covers for a journal
- How to decorate the covers with stamped paint designs
- How to bind the covers to a notepad

WHAT YOU'LL NEED . . . .

CLAY (TOP LAYER)

- approximately 6 oz (170 g) Kato Polyclay in the following colors:

    2½ oz (71 g) purple

    2 oz (56 g) copper

    ½ oz (14 g) gold

    ½ oz (14 g) white

    ¼ oz (7 g) black

    ¼ oz (7 g) magenta

(BACKING)

- 2 oz (56 g) gold
- 2 oz (56 g) purple

TOOLS

- craft knife
- small circle cutter
- brushes
- cosmetic sponges
- hand drill

OTHER MATERIALS

- white, burnt umber, sage green, brick, and gold acrylic paint
- wire-bound journal
- assorted stamps
- large tiles with a smooth surface
- ⁵⁄₁₆" (7.8 mm) dowel
- ⅜" (1 cm) dowel
- 5 yd (4.6 m) waxed linen
- clear nail polish

How to Make a Stamped Journal Cover

1 Take the wire binding off the journal. Trace the cover onto a piece of paper. Make a Skinner blend in approximately the setup shown in the photo. It is not necessary to make it exact. All the colors will blend into an interesting mix. Roll the Skinner blend out as wide as the machine permits.

(continued)

1

Stamped Journal Cover *continued*

2 Once the blend is complete, cut it in half lengthwise. One half will be used for the front cover, the other for the back.

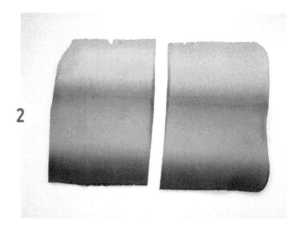

3 Roll one piece once through the machine on the third-thickest setting to increase the width of the blend with the stripes flowing in the same direction as before. Turn the blend sideways and roll the clay through at the fifth-thickest setting on the machine. Repeat for the second piece.

4 Lay one piece of clay on the paper inside the shape traced in step 1. Gently stretch the clay to fit the shape. Hold the clay with one hand and stroke the clay to stretch it. Stretch it gradually, or it will rip. Cut the clay to fit the shape of the cover.

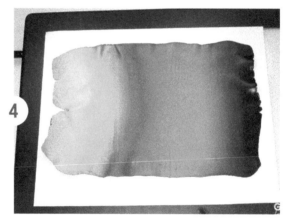

5 There is no right or wrong way to apply painted designs. Start with some brush strokes.

TIP The paint does not need to dry between coats, but if a mistake is made and the rest of the paint is dry, it's easier to remove the new paint with a wet paper towel if everything else is dry.

6 Apply paint to rubber stamps by dabbing the cosmetic sponges into the paint and applying the paint lightly to the stamp. Press the stamp onto the clay immediately—acrylic paint dries quickly.

7 When the clay has several layers of stamped images, let the paint dry. Continue with the same technique on the other piece of clay.

8 Roll out the purple and gold clay and make a large Skinner blend. The clay should be rolled out on the fourth or fifth setting of the pasta machine. When joined together, this piece of clay will add weight and strength to the cover. Cut the sheet in half, to the same dimensions as the covers.

9 Paint liquid polymer clay on the back of the cover sheet and lay the purple sheet on top. Slowly smooth the clay from one end to the other to avoid trapping air bubbles. Use a very small pin to prick holes if you find air bubbles. Repeat for the other cover.

(continued)

7

8

6

9

Stamped Journal Cover continued

10 Decide which piece of clay should be the front cover and which should be the back. Place the original journal cover on top of the clay and cut holes in the clay that align to holes in the cover. You only need enough holes to hold the covers together. Use a craft knife to cut the holes and follow with a small circle cutter to even them out.

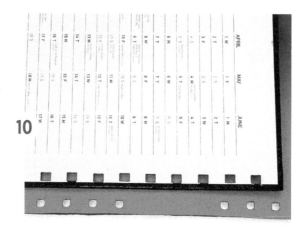

11 Bake the covers at 275°F (135°C) for 30 minutes on the paper and tented with foil. If using Kato clay, bake at 300°F (148°C) for strength.

TIP Sometimes acrylic paints will change color slightly due to the heat. Paint the colors on a little strip and bake to test the colors, especially if curing at 300°F (148°C).

12 When the clay has finished curing, wait a minute and then put the warm clay, with the paper underneath, on something very smooth and cool, such as a large tile. Cover the clay with another piece of paper and another tile. (A granite counter top and a heavy cookie sheet would work well.) Let the clay cool.

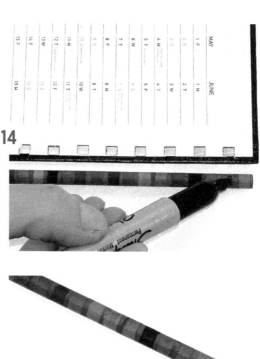

13 Sand the insides of the sheets and the edges lightly with 600-grit sandpaper to remove shiny spots and small imperfections.

14 Cut a 5⁄16" (7.8 mm) dowel to the same length as the cover. Paint the dowel with the same colors as the cover. Let the dowel dry. Place the dowel on the edge of the journal cover to mark the first hole for the binder.

15 Mark the dowel at the first top hole and the last bottom hole. Use a hand drill to make the holes.

16 Put the book together with waxed linen. Cut pieces of linen about 12" (30.5 cm) in length. Cut as many pieces as there are holes in the clay covers. Double the linen and feed it through the holes on either side of the journal and all the pages. Lay a ⅜" *(1 cm) dowel* down the middle of the binding area. Make a square knot with each section of linen over the ⅜" (1 cm) dowel.

17 Align the painted dowel to the bound edge. At the top and bottom knots, run the linen ends through the drilled hole in the dowel.

18 Cross the linen around and under the dowel. Bring the ends back up to the top of the dowel and make a square knot. Knot all the other ends around the dowel and cut them off at about ¼" (6 mm).

19 Dab a small dot of nail polish on knots and let it dry. Slide the ⅜" (1 cm) dowel out and your journal cover is complete.

QUICK REFERENCE
⅜" (1 cm) dowel. This dowel is not permanent; its placement is just to give the right amount of space for knotting the thread.

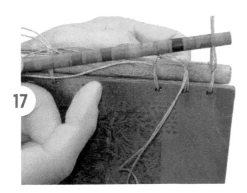

16

17

18

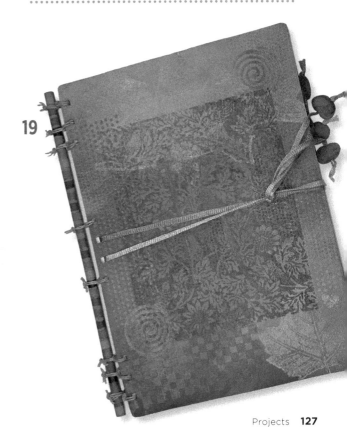

19

Metal Leaf Reversible Bracelet

Yes, you can use gold and silver leaf with polymer clay and get fantastic results. The metal leaf adheres to uncured clay with no need for adhesives, so there's less mess and no waiting. You can just keep crafting! After applying the metal leaf, the segments of this bracelet are covered with translucent polymer clay that protects the leaf and adds remarkable depth. One of the great things about translucent clay is the excellent shine that comes with sanding and buffing.

WHAT YOU'LL LEARN...............

- How to work with metal leaf
- How to apply translucent clay as a protective sheet
- How to make channels for stringing

WHAT YOU'LL NEED...............

CLAY

- 2 oz (56 g) black Kato clay
- red mixture:

    1¾ oz (49 g) red clay

    one piece black
- 2 oz (56 g) translucent clay
- 2 oz (56 g) scrap clay

TOOLS

- craft knife
- tissue blade
- ruler
- pencil

OTHER MATERIALS

- metal leaf in silver and gold
- one sheet graph paper
- 24" (61 cm) 0.7-mm stretch plastic

How to Make a Metal Leaf Bracelet

1 To make a paper template for the bracelet segments, fold a section of graph paper in half following a line exactly. Draw half of a curved rectangular shape along the fold.

(continued)

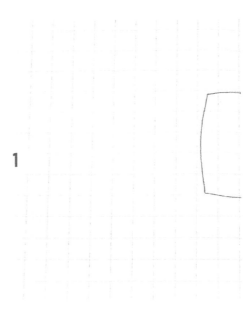

1

Metal Leaf Bracelet *continued*

2 Cut out both sides with the paper still folded in half.

TIP Cutting half shapes from folded paper always results in a perfectly symmetrical whole shape from one side to the other.

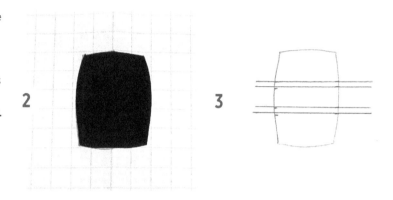

3 Use the hole created in the graph paper to trace the shape onto an index card or postcard. With a pencil and ruler, divide the shape into thirds. Draw a line ⅟₁₆" (1.6 mm) below the top line and another ⅟₁₆" (1.6 mm) above the bottom line. Draw the marks out further than the shape so when the shape is cut out of the card, the marks are still visible. Cut this shape out with a craft knife.

4 Condition both the black and red clay and roll each of them out to the thickest setting on the pasta machine. Cut a section from the black clay about 3" (7.6 cm) square. Open the gold leaf package, separate the sheets, and carefully lay the clay on a sheet of gold leaf.

5 When you pull the clay away from the leaf, the leaf should rip and leave the rest of the sheet in the package.

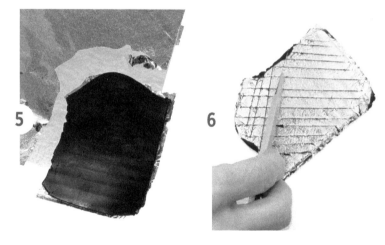

6 Remove any residue of the gold leaf from the edges of the clay. Place a protective tissue paper sheet over the gold leaf and smooth the leaf down with your fingers. With a craft knife, cut shallow diagonal slits in the clay, cutting just through the leaf and a small amount of clay.

7 Roll the sheet through the pasta machine to the fourth setting. Set the clay aside.

8 Roll 1 oz (28 g) of translucent clay with a hand roller to about the thickest setting of the pasta machine.

9 Roll the translucent clay through the pasta machine on the sixth-thinnest setting. Cut a section of the translucent clay large enough to fit over the black clay.

10 Lay the translucent clay over the foiled clay and roll through the pasta machine on the fourth-thinnest setting. The translucent clay should be joined to the foiled clay with all the air rolled out from between the two sheets of clay.

(continued)

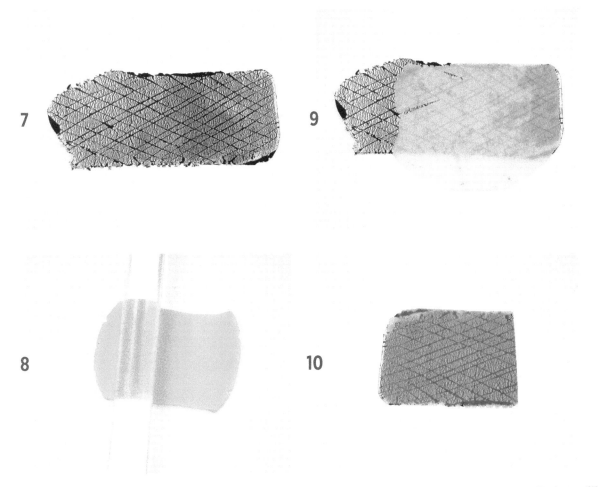

7

9

8

10

Metal Leaf Bracelet continued

11 Repeat steps 4 to 10 to make enough beads for your bracelet. Then, repeat steps 4 to 10, using the silver leaf with the red clay, making the same number of pieces.

12 With a template in place, use a craft knife to cut a shape from the black foiled clay.

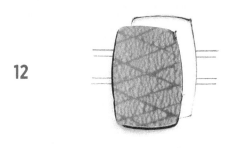

12

13 Roll out the scrap clay to the fourth setting on the pasta machine and use the template and the craft knife to cut a shape the same size as the black shape. Lay the scrap shape on top of the template and cut across all the lines drawn on the template. The two ¹⁄₁₆" (1.6 mm) sections will be put in the scrap pile.

13

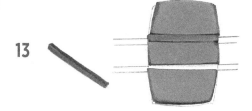

14 Lay the three sections of scrap clay over the back of one bracelet segment. Align the outer edges, leaving spaces at the two one-third marks.

15 Put the other color clay shape on the top of the scrap to make a clay sandwich. Place an index card over the shape and gently press the edges to join the layers together. Before baking, make sure the holes are not covered with clay. Bake the sections at the clay manufacturer's specified temperature for 30 minutes. When the sections have cured and cooled, sand them so they are quite smooth.

14

16 Roll out some black clay to the fifth setting on the pasta machine. With a tissue blade, cut strips the width of the side of the clay bead. Coat the sides of the sections with liquid polymer clay.

16

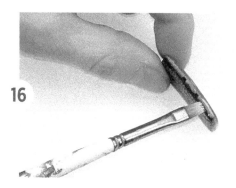

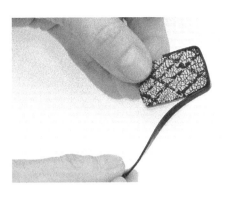

17 Add the strips around the edge of the bead.

18 Poke holes through the side strips where the string will go.

19 Use a tissue blade to cut the excess clay from the edge of the bead.

20 Bake the beads on an index card at the clay manufacturer's specified temperature for another 20 minutes. The translucent clay should be very clear. If not, use a heat gun to clear the clay. Aim the gun at the bead and move slightly back and forth about 5" (12.7 cm) away from the surface of the clay. Heat guns can get very hot, so keep an eye on the clay and make sure it doesn't start to burn.

21 String the beads on stretchy elastic. Tie a surgeon's knot in the elastic and then apply a small drop of nail polish to the knots.

17

18

19

21

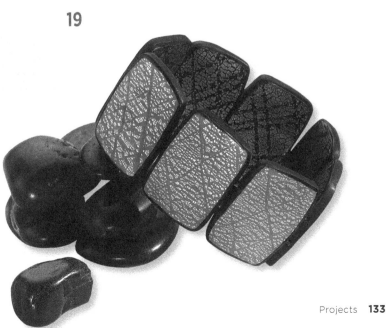

Mokume-Gane Picture Frame

Mokume-Gane (pronounced Mo-KOO-may GAH-nay) is a metalsmithing technique that originated 300 years ago in Japan. Various metals were bonded together using heat and pressure, then carved and filed to show the patterns inside. These metal laminates were originally used to embellish samurai swords.

In the polymer clay version of the technique, stacks of clay are manipulated with stamps or texture tools. The patterns that are revealed when you slice into the stack can be used for a variety of projects.

WHAT YOU'LL LEARN . . . .

- How to imitate the Mokume-Gane technique using stacks of polymer clay
- How to use household materials to create unique patterns
- How to make use of non-oven-safe surfaces in polymer clay designs

WHAT YOU'LL NEED . . . .

CLAY

- Premo clay or clay of choice:
- 3 oz (85 g) black
- 1 oz (28 g) pearl
- 1 oz (28 g) translucent clay
- 1 oz (28 g) red mixture:

    seven parts cadmium red

    one part black

TOOLS

- texture tools, such as a wavy blade, Kemper or cookie cutters, blunt end of paintbrush, plastic fork, bottle cap, etc.
- sharp tissue blade

OTHER MATERIALS

- silver leaf
- frame with wide, flat border (does not need to be oven-safe)
- cyanoacrylate glue
- clay-compatible glaze, such as Studio by Sculpey Glossy Glaze

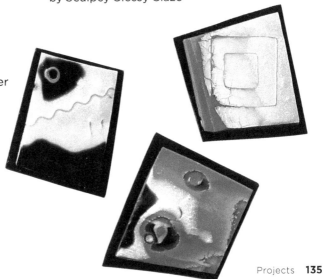

How to Make a Mokume-Gane Picture Frame

1 Condition 1 oz (28 g) of each color of clay, then roll the black, red, and pearl clay sheets out to the pasta machine's thickest setting. Roll the translucent clay to a thin setting. Trim the sheets to roughly similar-sized rectangles, reserving the cut-off edges for later.

2 Open the package of silver leaf, carefully peeling the paper away from the leaf. Press the sheet of translucent clay onto the silver leaf. Tear or cut excess leaf from around the clay.

3 Stack the clay sheets, pressing them to bind them together and eliminate air bubbles.

4 Use a clay blade to cut the stack in half, then stack one half on top of the other. Compress. Repeat to create as many layers as needed. More layers and more compressing generally lead to a larger variety of colors in each slice.

5 Using the scraps from the first step, roll small balls of clay and press them into the bottom of the stack. These will create round areas of color in the Mokume-Gane stack.

6 Press texture tools into the top of the clay stack. The dull end of a paintbrush will create a rounded area of color. A wavy clay blade pressed partially through the stack will create a ripple pattern. The tongs of a plastic fork can be used to drag lines in the clay. Cookie or Kemper cutters create interesting shapes. The texture options are limited only by your imagination—try bamboo skewers or chopsticks, drinking straws, leather tools, pen caps, pencils, rubber stamps, and texture sheets.

TIP Carefully press the dull edge of tools, such as the wavy blade, into the stack. Dull edges create a better impression than sharp edges, which tend to cut through the clay without dragging the color.

7 Roll thin snakes from the scrap clay. Press them into the rounded holes you created. Compress the stack, pushing in the top and edges to fill in any gaps.

8 Allow the clay to rest until cool. You can speed this process by placing it in the refrigerator. Once it's ready, use a sharp tissue blade to slice thin layers off the top of the clay stack, revealing the patterns inside. Cutting thin, even slices may be important for some Mokume-Gane projects, but it's not essential here. Lay the slices on a sheet of wax paper while you continue to work.

TIP There are a variety of ways to slice layers off of a Mokume-Gane stack. Place the stack against something heavy so it doesn't move while you work. Some people find putting the clay on a rounded surface, such as a jar, makes it easier to get thin slices. You may prefer to turn the stack on its edge and slice it like a cane. Whichever method you use, be sure to clean the clay blade regularly as you work to prevent drag. If the blade does get stuck, ease it back and forth in a gentle sawing motion.

(continued)

5
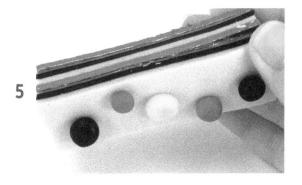

6

7

8

Mokume-Gane Picture Frame *continued*

9 Look at both sides of each slice to see which pattern you prefer. If you have any uneven or thick pieces, you can run them through the pasta machine to make them even. Cut the slices into small shapes (smaller than the frame's borders) with interesting designs.

10 Roll out 2 oz (56 g) of black clay into a medium thickness sheet. Place the Mokume-Gane slices on the black sheet. Trim around each piece to create a framed effect. Bake the pieces.

11 Sand and buff the pieces if desired, then glaze them to protect the silver leaf. Lay the clay pieces around the frame border until you find a pleasing arrangement. Use cyanoacrylate glue to adhere the pieces to the frame, holding them in place until they are set. If you find you have empty spots, you can repeat step 10 to frame solid colors of clay. You could also add silver leaf to a strip of black clay, then frame it to create metallic highlights.

9

10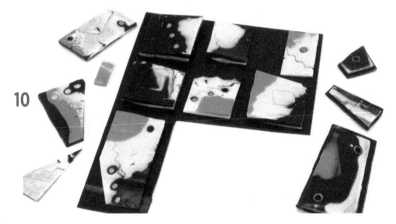

11

Variations

This frame shows translucent clay tinted with small amounts of colored clay to create depth. Since the metal frame used for its base is oven-safe, the clay was glued directly onto the frame with white glue before baking.

Make a pen with scraps from the frame project. Press small pieces into a black background for a Mokume-Gane pen, or twist the scraps together for a marbled pen. Using pen kits with polymer clay creates professional-looking pens. A matching frame and pen would make a great gift!

Name Tag with Embedded Pin

Embedding objects in polymer clay can be both functional and fun. While some glues do work with polymer clay, embedding jewelry findings directly into the clay often adds strength while giving the piece a more finished look. This name tag uses a layer of textured clay to hide and secure the pinback. It also makes use of a two-part silicone mold putty that is handy for creating molds of softer items, like the ribbon rose that gives the name tag its cakelike appearance.

WHAT YOU'LL LEARN . . . .

- How to use Amazing Mold Putty to make a reusable silicone mold
- How to use a silicone mold with clay
- How to trace a design using extruded clay
- How to embed a pinback into a polymer clay piece

WHAT YOU'LL NEED . . . .

CLAY

- brown mixture:

    1 oz (28 g) burnt umber

    ¼ ounce (7 g) ultramarine blue

    ⅛ oz (4 g) black

- yellow mixture:

    ½ oz (14 g) white

    ⅛ oz (4 g) zinc yellow

- green mixture:

    ¼ oz (7 g) green

    ⅛ oz (4 g) white

    1⁄16 oz (2 g) raw sienna

TOOLS

- clay blade and/or cookie cutter
- scissors
- pen or blunt tool
- clay extruder
- needle tool
- texture sheet, such as Parallel Lines by Shade-Tex

OTHER MATERIALS

- Amazing Mold Putty
- ribbon rose
- name, printed out or handwritten on paper
- Kato Clear Medium Liquid Polyclay
- ¾" (1.9 cm) pinback jewelry finding

How to Make a Name Tag with Embedded Pin

1 Measure out equal amounts of white and yellow from the Amazing Mold Putty containers. Mix them together until the color is consistent with no marbling. Roll the putty into a smooth ball, applying pressure to eliminate any creases.

2 Cut off one ribbon rose and press it into the mold putty mixture until the back of the rose is even with the top of the putty ball. Leave the rose in place, and let the mold set for 30 minutes.

3 Once the mold is set, remove the rose. Press small balls of the conditioned yellow clay mixture into the mold to create six yellow roses.

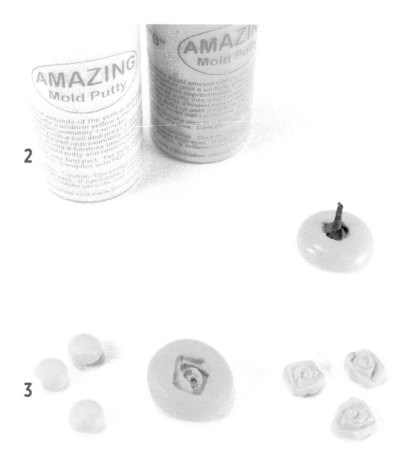

4 Condition the brown clay mixture and roll out to the thickest or second-thickest pasta machine setting. Use a cookie cutter or clay blade to cut out a rectangle 3" wide × 2" tall (7.6 × 5 cm). Write your name on scrap paper as you want it to appear, or use a word processing program to print your name in a favorite font. Cut out around your name and center it on the clay sheet, then use a pen or other blunt tool to trace the letters onto the clay surface. The goal is to leave a slight indention to use as a pattern for the extruded writing. Remove the paper and bake the name tag according to the clay manufacturer's instructions.

5 Once the clay has cooled, spread a light layer of liquid polymer clay to cover the entire top of the name tag. The liquid polymer clay will help the extruded clay letters stay in place, and it will give the final name tag a nice finished surface.

(continued)

4

5

TIP To use a silicone mold, first roll the clay into a smooth ball to eliminate creases. If the mold has deep areas, shape the clay into a cone and press the point of the clay into the deepest part of the mold.

Overfilling a mold will create a visible edge, and underfilling it may create a weaker piece that is missing details.

Determine the right amount of clay to use by pressing a clay ball into the mold, then using a clay blade to slice the excess clay off the top of the mold. Pop the clay out of the mold and roll it back into a ball to determine its size. Making each ball of clay that same size ensures identical molded images

Silicone molds generally don't stick to the clay, but if you have an especially detailed mold, you may find it useful to spritz it with water for an easier release.

6 Roll the remaining yellow clay mixture into a cylinder and place it in the barrel of the clay extruder. Use the smallest round disk to extrude a long clay snake. Or, if you don't have an extruder, roll out a thin clay snake. Fill the indented lines on the name tag with the extruded clay, using a clay blade to make cuts at the beginning and end of each letter.

6

7 Place yellow roses in the name tag's corners. Pinch off tiny bits of the green clay mixture and shape each one into a pointed leaf. Use a needle tool to press a vein line in the middle of each leaf, then attach it to the clay between the roses. Use one of the small round extruder disks to press out brown clay, then twist the extruded snakes together to form a border for the edge of the name tag. Bake according to the clay manufacturer's instructions.

7

8 Roll the remaining brown clay mixture to a thin sheet on the pasta machine. Cut out a piece that is slightly larger than the pinback finding. Spread a little liquid polymer clay on the back of the name tag where you want the pinback to go. Smooth the thin brown sheet onto the liquid polymer clay, then press the open pinback on top.

8

9 Roll out a medium thickness sheet of brown clay on the pasta machine. Press a *texture sheet* into the clay, then cut out a ¾" (1.9 cm) square.

10 Glue the textured clay piece on top of the pinback with liquid polymer clay, without getting clay or liquid polymer clay in the pin closure. Carefully test to be sure the pin still opens and closes freely. Bake the name tag according to the clay manufacturer's instructions. If you want a glossy finish, you can heat up the top layer of liquid polymer clay with a heat embossing gun immediately after baking. Otherwise, leave it as is for a matte look.

10

QUICK REFERENCE

Texture sheets are available in a wide variety of patterns, or you can make your own using silicone putty or polymer clay. Flexible texture sheets may not require a release agent, but it's usually best to spray plastic sheets with water first to prevent the clay from sticking. Use your fingers or a roller to press the texture sheet into the clay.

Variations

Try molding a variety of other items for your name tag, such as buttons, shells, or charms. This name tag uses a toner transfer (see "Transfers" page 178) instead of extruded letters. You could also use rubber stamps for the letters.

Buttons with Embedded Shanks

As my seamstress mother says, "The buttons make the outfit." Polymer clay's color-matching capabilities make it ideal for creating one-of-a-kind buttons to customize handmade or store-bought clothes. Select print fabrics that have small patterns and good contrast. The metal frame and UV resin add a sophisticated touch. These buttons will definitely make your outfits extra-special!

WHAT YOU'LL LEARN . . . .

- How to coat fabric with liquid polymer clay
- How to embed a jump ring in clay to act as a button shank
- How to use UV resin with polymer clay

WHAT YOU'LL NEED . . . .

CLAY

- ½ oz (14 g) Premo! Orange (or clay of choice in a color that matches your fabric)

TOOLS

- small sheet of glass or a ceramic tile
- pen or pencil
- scissors
- ¾" (1.9 cm) round cookie cutter
- heat embossing gun

- needle-nose pliers (optional)

OTHER MATERIALS

- fabric
- liquid polymer clay
- jewelry findings, such as 16-mm wire shape, circle loop, or jump ring
- 6 mm jump ring
- Lisa Pavelka's Magic-Glos Dimensional Gloss UV Resin

How to Make Buttons with Embedded Shanks

1 Iron the fabric if necessary to eliminate major wrinkles, then cut a strip large enough to make several buttons. Spread a thin layer of liquid polymer clay across a ceramic tile or a small sheet of glass. The liquid polymer clay should cover an area a little larger than your fabric piece. Place the fabric in the liquid polymer clay, pressing out air bubbles with your fingers, starting in the middle and moving toward the edges. Apply a layer of liquid polymer clay on top of the fabric. Let it penetrate the fabric for a few minutes, then add more if necessary. Bake according to the liquid polymer clay instructions.

(continued)

TIP If you use a small sheet of glass for the prep and baking surface, you can easily lift the glass and peek underneath to check for bubbles.

1

Buttons with Embedded Shanks *continued*

2 Trace the *jewelry finding* onto the back side of the cooled fabric with a pen or pencil. Use scissors to cut out as many fabric circles as you want for buttons.

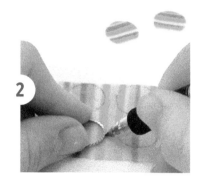

QUICK REFERENCE

Jewelry finding. Browse the jewelry findings section of your local craft store for round metal shapes to frame the fabric on top of the buttons. Wire shapes and circle loops are both closed metal loops, while a jump ring has a small gap in one side. Any will work for the buttons, though you may want to use clay to hide the gap in the jump ring.

3 Roll out conditioned clay to the thickest pasta machine setting. Place it flat on the work surface and spread a layer of liquid polymer clay over it. Then press a fabric circle into the clay. Press the metal jewelry finding down on top of the fabric. Center the cookie cutter over the design; then cut through the clay to create a button. Smooth the top edges of the clay up around the jewelry finding to secure the metal in place and give the button a rounded look.

4 Turn the button over and cut a narrow slit in center back of clay. Use pliers to press a 6-mm jump ring, gapped edge first, about halfway into the clay slit. Smooth the clay to cover the slit. Next, add a clay strip to reinforce the button shank. On a medium setting, roll out matching or contrasting clay. Cut a strip that is narrower than the inside of the jump ring. Feed the clay strip through the jump ring, using liquid polymer clay as a glue, then press it down on both ends. Add texture with a needle tool if desired. Bake face down on an index card.

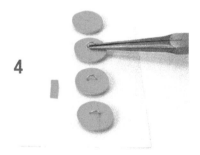

TIP For patterned fabric, line up the buttons so the design goes the same direction on all of them before cutting the slits in back. This ensures your finished buttons will match.

5 Press a ball of scrap clay onto a ceramic tile, then press the button shank into the clay to hold it level. Apply Magic-Glos UV resin on top of the fabric, beginning with the inner edges of the metal, and then fill the gaps in the middle. Allow the resin to level. If it pulls away from the edges, add one additional drop to the middle, and allow it to spread to the edges. The applicator tip or a toothpick can help direct the flow of the resin. Wipe away any drips with a paper towel, using a little rubbing alcohol to remove any residue.

6 If there are tiny bubbles in the resin, use a heat embossing gun to pop them before curing. First, point the gun away from the project, so dust trapped in the gun won't blow into the resin, and turn it on. Hold the gun a couple of inches (5 cm) above the button, and direct the air at the bubbles in the resin for a few seconds. They should pop quickly. Don't hold the gun too close to the resin, or leave it in one place for too long, because the clay could burn or the resin could overflow.

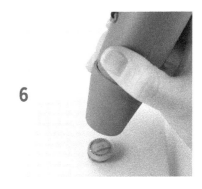

6

7 Cure the resin. Magic-Glos is a UV resin, which means you can cure it in sunlight. This generally takes 15 minutes in full sun, or longer on partially cloudy days. If you're curing the items outdoors and are concerned about wind blowing dust into your project, invert a drinking glass or glass bowl on top. If you prefer to cure indoors, UV nail lamps will also do the job.

Once the first resin layer is cured, you may choose to add additional layers for a more domed surface. Add one drop at a time to the middle until you are happy with the results. Cure again after each layer.

7

TIP It takes just the right touch to get your Magic-Glos layer thick enough to reach the edges, but not so thick that it goes over the edges. If you've never used Magic-Glos (or other resins) before, you may want to practice on a scrap piece first to get a feel for it. You can always add another layer of Magic-Glos after curing if the first layer pulls back from the edges.

Variations

Combine a variety of fabrics with a variety of clay colors for lots of button-y fun!

Embed post earring backs instead of a button shank, and you can make earrings to match your outfit. Try scrapbooking paper instead of fabric for another great look.

STEAMPUNK-STYLE JEWELRY   Jean Campbell

JEWELRY ARTS WORKSHOP   Pure Silver   Metal Clay Beads   Linda Kaye-Moses

Polymer Clay and Mixed Media together at last   Christi Friesen

Wool Toys & Friends   Step-by-Step Instructions for Needle-Felting Fun   Sharp

The Complete Photo Guide to PAPER CRAFTS   Boerens

Magnetic Word Stones

Polymer clay has an amazing ability to mimic other materials. If you like the look of natural stone, you may find that polymer clay's comparative lightness and malleability give it a big advantage over the real thing in craft projects. By varying the inclusions, shapes, and finishes, you can create a wide variety of stones from polymer clay.

Polished stones with engraved words can be beautiful and inspirational. While rubber stamps work great, you can also cut costs and get creative by making your own stamped messages from clay. Embedding a powerful magnet inside gives the clay stone hidden holding power that would make an actual stone jealous.

WHAT YOU'LL LEARN.............................

- How to make your own word stamps to use with polymer clay
- How to create a faux stone effect using embossing powders and translucent clay
- How to hide a magnet inside a polymer clay piece
- How to create a glossy finish using liquid polymer clay

WHAT YOU'LL NEED.............................

CLAY

- ½ oz (14 g) Premo! Frost or other translucent clay
- a small amount of scrap clay (any color)

TOOLS

- scissors
- tissue blade
- clay extruder and smallest disk
- craft knife
- water spritzer
- toothbrush or stiff-bristled brush
- heat embossing gun

OTHER MATERIALS

- printout of word in mirror image
- Sculpey Bake & Bond Bakeable Adhesive, optional
- Ranger Embossing Antiquities (Verdigris)
- ¼" (6 mm) power magnet
- black acrylic paint
- paper towels
- liquid polymer clay
- rubbing alcohol

How to Make Magnetic Word Stones

1 Start by making a custom word stamp. Use a computer to print the chosen word in mirror image. While any font will work, you may wish to start with a sans-serif font with simple lines. Increasing the scaling and kerning to create more space between letters will make it easier to trace the letters of the stamp. If your computer will not print in mirror image, you can print as usual and do an image transfer instead (see "Transfer" page 178). Cut out the printed word.

(continued)

1

Magnetic Word Stones continued

2 Roll scrap clay to the pasta machine's thickest setting. Spread *Bake & Bond* adhesive evenly across the sheet, then press the paper onto the adhesive, printed side up. Trim the clay sheet's edges to be slightly larger than the paper. With the paper glued in place, bake for 15 minutes.

3 Use the clay extruder's smallest disk to create a thin clay snake. Spread more Bake & Bond or liquid polymer clay on top of the sheet of paper. This may smear some types of ink, which is fine as long as you can still see the letters. Follow the lines of the letters with the extruded clay, using a clay blade or needle tool to help shape the letters and trim the ends. Bake the stamp.

4 Condition translucent clay, then form into a flat disk. Pour ¼ to ½ teaspoon of the embossing powder into the middle of the disk, then fold it in half to trap the powder. Continue working with the clay until the powder is mixed in completely, and shape the clay into an oval with a flat surface large enough for the word stamp.

5 Press a power magnet into the center of the stone's back, stopping as soon as the magnet is even with the clay. Nudge a thin layer of clay to cover the magnet, then eliminate any seams. Don't bury the magnet too deep inside the clay, as this may weaken the magnet's holding power.

2

3

4

QUICK REFERENCE

Bake & Bond is a bakeable adhesive that is thicker than liquid polymer clay. It works especially well for adhering polymer clay to other materials, like paper or wood. If you don't have Bake & Bond, substitute liquid polymer clay or white glue.

5
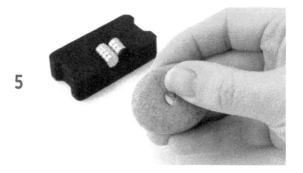

6 Spritz the top of the stone with water, then press the word stamp into the clay. Remove the stamp and check the impression. Use your finger to smooth any unwanted lines from the stamp's edges. Fix any incomplete stamped areas with a needle tool, and then bake the stone.

7 When the clay is cool, use a toothbrush or a paintbrush to push black paint into the grooves. Wipe away excess paint on the surface with a paper towel. Clean off any unwanted paint that dries on the clay's surface with rubbing alcohol and a paper towel.

8 Use your finger or a paintbrush to apply a layer of liquid polymer clay to the bottom and sides of the stone. Cure the liquid polymer clay by holding a heat embossing gun about an inch (2.5 cm) from the clay for one or two minutes. The liquid polymer clay will start out looking wet, then become dull and cloudy before returning to a shiny finish. Keep the heat gun moving to avoid burning any one area. Once the back and sides are cool, follow the same steps to add liquid polymer clay to the stone's top.

TIP While Translucent Liquid Sculpey (TLS) and Kato Liquid Polyclay can be used interchangeably in many projects, TLS will not cure to a clear glossy finish. Use Kato Liquid Polyclay for the best results.

Variations

Try different colors of embossing powder for different effects. Ranger's Enamelware Embossing Powder or Cement Embossing Antiquities create light or dark gray rocks, and Ranger's Ocher Embossing Antiquities creates a light brown rock. Add black or white embossing powders to create your own custom blend, or tint any mixture with a couple of drops of alcohol ink.

Extruded Clay Votive Holder

A clay extruder, or clay gun, presses clay through a disk to create snakes and other shapes. Different brands and styles are available, ranging from the cheap plunger-style extruder to the more expensive (but much easier to use) screw-top extruder. While it is possible to create any of these shapes by hand, the extruder tool is good for creating lots of very even shapes very quickly, making techniques like the one in this chapter possible.

A simple glass votive holder becomes a work of art when it's covered with spirals of blended color. The clay is translucent, lightly tinted so the candle inside will shine through and create beautiful shadows. The project can be time-consuming; however the technique is simple and repetitive, so many people find it to be meditative.

WHAT YOU'LL LEARN...

- How to tint translucent clay while preserving its clarity
- How to stack clay in an extruder to create gradated extrusions
- How to make clay spirals

WHAT YOU'LL NEED...

CLAY

- ½ oz (14 g) frost or translucent
- red mixture:
    - ½ oz (14 g) frost or translucent
    - 1/16 oz (2 g) cadmium red
    - one large pea-sized ball burnt umber
- orange mixture:
    - ½ oz (14 g) frost or translucent
    - 1/16 oz (2 g) orange
    - one pinch cadmium yellow
    - one pinch burnt umber

- green mixture:
    - ½ oz (14 g) frost or translucent
    - 1/16 oz (2 g) green
    - 1/16 oz (2 g) cadmium yellow
    - one large pea-sized ball burnt umber
- brown mixture:
    - ½ oz (14 g) frost or translucent
    - one large pea-sized ball burnt umber
    - one large pea-sized ball raw sienna

TOOLS

- clay extruder
- clay blade and/or craft knife
- ceramic tile
- needle tool
- clay scraper, optional

OTHER MATERIALS

- small glass votive holder
- liquid polymer clay

How to Make an Extruded Clay Votive Holder

1 Rub a light layer of liquid polymer clay over the outside of the votive holder. This will help the polymer clay adhere to the glass.

2 Roll the translucent clay out to the pasta machine's thinnest setting. Wrap the clay around the votive holder, using a needle tool to pop any air bubbles. Trim the top and bottom edges by running your clay blade around the edge at an angle.

3 Condition the red, orange, brown, and green clay mixtures. Roll each color into a log the same diameter as the extruder's barrel. Cut off a ½" (1.3 cm) slice of each color and stack them together as shown. Press the stack into the barrel. Use the medium circle disk with twelve holes to extrude the clay, allowing the individual snakes to drape separately across your work surface so they don't stick together.

TIP Extrude only as many snakes as you can use at one time. Extruded snakes tend to become brittle as the conditioned clay gets cold. It's much easier to spiral snakes without breaking them if they are freshly extruded.

To vary the appearance, adjust the thickness of the color layers. For thinner layers, choose a disk with fewer holes to compensate for the shorter stack. The colors will blend quicker and more completely in the resulting snake to create a more muted look. Including both types of spirals adds an interesting variation to the votive holder.

4 Roll about half of the extruded snakes into spirals; begin at alternating ends of the gradation to vary the look. To start a spiral, hold one end of the snake on your fingertip while you pull the rest of the snake around it with your other hand.

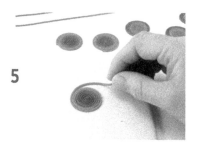

5 Once the spiral is started, you can place it on your work surface and continue to make the spiral, circling around until you reach the end of the clay snake.

6 Condition a ball of scrap clay and place it on a ceramic tile, then press the bottom of the votive holder firmly into the clay to secure the glass. Place two spirals on the votive holder, leaving some space between them. Add other extruded snakes, one at a time, to *extend the circles* until they intersect. Add more spirals and extending snakes. Cut some of the spirals in half and place them on the edge of the glass, carefully moving them from the work surface to the glass with a *clay scraper* or blade to prevent the cut spirals from falling apart.

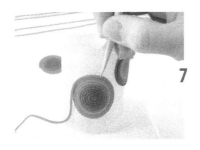

7 You can texture some snakes by pressing a needle tool or the dull edge of a craft knife into the clay. Try a variety of dots and dashes. It is easiest to texture a snake while it is the outermost snake in the spiral, before adding the next snake. Adding texture can also help the clay expand slightly to fill small gaps.

8 Fill any remaining smaller gaps with tiny balls of clay. Press the balls into place. Poke holes in the center with a needle tool if desired.

9 Trim the snakes at the top and bottom edges by running your clay blade around the edge of the glass at an angle. Add liquid polymer clay around the top edge. Extrude a large green clay snake and attach it around the top, smoothing the cut ends. Bake according to the clay manufacturer's instructions.

10 This technique looks especially nice when sanded and buffed to a glossy finish. Be careful not to sand too much at the coarser grits, as it might sand away the detail work.

QUICK REFERENCE

Extend the circles. You can use entire snakes to make a spiral bigger on all sides. If the spiral is close to an edge, cut small pieces to build up just one side. Use a clay blade or craft knife to make cuts, trying to leave as little space as possible between the cut edge and the snake beside it.

Clay scraper. A clay scraper is a very thin oval-shaped tool, usually made from aluminum. It is especially useful for sliding under sheets of uncured clay to move them.

Carved Faux Ivory Business Card Holder

The faux ivory makes this business card holder a great gift for men or women. Use a favorite font to carve a monogram, or base a carving on one of your own sketches. You could even make a gift for a friend with their company's logo carved into the front. Think of the compliments they'll receive every time they hand out a business card!

Working with cured clay can lead to exciting results. Carving after baking gives more control over the depth and neatness of the carving. And while it's possible to carve cured clay with a needle tool or knife, a lino cutting tool like the ones used to carve stamps is worth the small investment if you like the carved effect. Having the right tool makes the carving go faster, plus it's much easier on your hands. Cured clay is very easy to carve.

In addition to teaching carving, this project shows how to stretch stripes in faux ivory using a technique by Kathryn Jo Ottman. This method is handy anytime you want to lengthen a striped pattern.

WHAT YOU'LL LEARN

- How to make faux ivory
- How to lengthen a striped pattern using the pasta machine
- How to use a Speedball tool to carve cured polymer clay

WHAT YOU'LL NEED

CLAY

- white mixture:

    1 oz (28 g) white

    ½ oz (14 g) translucent

    ½ oz (14 g) ecru

- 1 oz (28 g) translucent

TOOLS

- pen
- clay blade
- clay scraper
- Speedball tool with V-shaped cutter #1 and/or #2
- toothbrush or stiff-bristled brush
- brayer or acrylic roller, optional

OTHER MATERIALS

- business card holder
- image or logo to carve, printed on copy paper (image shown is from *The Crafter's Pattern Sourcebook* by Mary MacCarthy)
- cyanoacrylate glue
- acrylic paint
- paper towel

How to Make a Carved Faux Ivory Business Card Holder

1 Condition and roll out the translucent clay and the white clay mixture to the fifth-thickest setting on the pasta machine. Cut eight 1" × 2" (2.5 × 5 cm) rectangles from each color. Create two stacks, alternating translucent and white in both up to eight stacked sheets. Trim off any uneven edges, then compress each stack gently with your hands or an acrylic roller.

2 Roll each stack through the pasta machine at its thickest setting to create two compressed sheets with very thin stripes.

3 Trim each sheet's edges, then stack one on top of the other. Be careful to alternate the colors. You should now have sixteen stripes. Cut in half and stack again to get thirty-two stripes.

4 Roll the leftover translucent clay from previous steps to the thickest setting of the pasta machine. The sheet needs to be as wide as the business card holder and at least half as tall. Trim the top edge and sides to straighten.

Cut slices from the side of the striped stack and place them along the top edge of the translucent sheet. Alternate between white and translucent stripes as you place the slices. Continue until you have striped pieces all the way across.

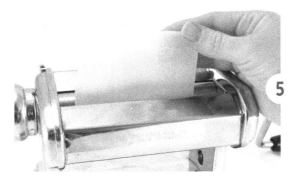

5 Place the translucent sheet in the pasta machine at the thickest setting, lining up the striped edge so it touches the rollers. Roll the sheet through to elongate the stripes. Trim off any unstriped clay from the bottom of the sheet. Stack it under the striped clay, lining it up at the top edge for another pass through the pasta machine at the thickest setting. Move the pasta machine to its second-thickest setting. Run the sheet through again in the same direction. Run the sheet through at thinner settings until the stripes are long enough to cover the front of the business card holder.

6 Mix the remaining white clay with any striped or translucent scraps you cut off in the previous steps. Roll out this scrap clay mixture to the first or second pasta machine setting. The sheet needs to be as big as the front of the business card holder. Layer the striped ivory sheet on top of this sheet and press them together to make a thick sheet for carving. Use the business card holder as a template, placing it upside down on top of this combined sheet. Cut the sheet to size.

7 Place the image you plan to carve, printed side up, on the clay sheet. Trace the pattern with a pen or other blunt-edged tool. Leave a slight indentation, enough to follow during the carving step.

8 Trim the edges of the clay sheet, holding your clay blade at an angle to create a slight bevel. Bake the clay sheet, still on the business card holder, according to the clay manufacturer's instructions.

(continued)

Carved Faux Ivory Business Card Holder *continued*

9 Allow the clay to cool, then *carve the image* using a Speedball carving tool with V-shaped cutter tip #1 or #2. Use the indented areas as a guide for carving, referring to the printed image if there are areas where the lines are unclear. You shouldn't need to apply much pressure, just guide the tool along the indented lines, allowing the tool to slide through the clay. Getting a smooth cut is more important than following the lines exactly. You can also freehand carve additional designs or borders.

9

QUICK REFERENCE

Carve the image. Follow these tips for carving:

• Be sure to follow all safety warnings.

• Hold the tool either like a pen or with the ball in the palm of your hand, applying pressure above the blade with your index finger.

• Start by carving a very shallow line. If you want it deeper, make another pass. The more pressure you apply, the deeper and wider the cut.

• Rotate the piece as you carve so you don't have to keep adjusting your carving hand.

• Go slowly and take breaks. Hurrying can lead to mistakes or even injuries if the tool slips.

• Don't worry too much about nicks and small mistakes. Once you antique them, extra lines just add to the distressed look.

10

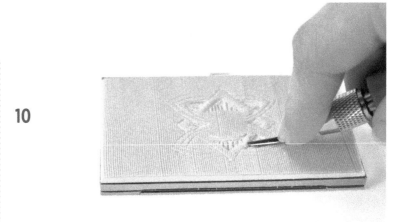

11

10 Some images have inset areas you can carve out to give the piece a more 3D look. To dig out a whole area, make multiple passes along the same lines, holding the carving tool at a slightly deeper angle for each pass. Carving with parallel lines gives the area a shaded look that will show up well when antiqued.

12

11 Some images also have areas that appear to be raised. Use liquid polymer clay to attach clay snakes or balls for added dimension, then bake the card holder again.

12 Carefully slide the edge of a clay blade or scraper underneath one edge of the clay sheet to pop the sheet off of the business card holder. With a stiff-bristled brush or toothbrush, push brown acrylic paint into the carved areas. Wipe excess paint off the surface with a clean paper towel.

13

13 Apply cyanoacrylate glue to the front of the business card holder, then center the clay sheet over the holder and press it in.

Variation

Add a faux wood background. Make and bake the wood background and the carved ivory topper separately, then sand and buff each part before gluing them together.

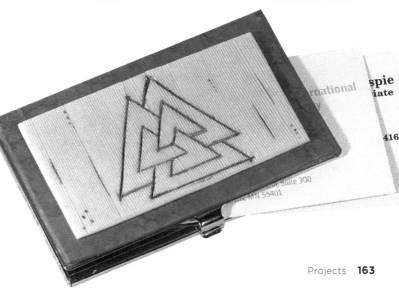

Inlay and Appliqué Magnetic Tic-Tac-Toe Game

Inlay is a technique often used in woodwork, in which pieces of a contrasting material are embedded into cutouts in a base material. Appliqué is a term usually used in quilting, where a small piece of fabric is stitched to the top of another fabric piece and the stitches are often part of the design. This project combines aspects of both of these techniques to create a colorful magnetic game tin, complete with coordinating game pieces.

WHAT YOU'LL LEARN . . . .

- How to cover a metal tin with polymer clay
- How to use nested cookie cutters to create an inlay effect
- How to enhance the look of clay appliqués with decorative "stitching"
- How to create magnetic game pieces that incorporate polymer clay, scrapbook paper, and resin

WHAT YOU'LL NEED . . . .

CLAY

- Studio by Sculpey or clay of choice:
- 1 oz (28 g) Spanish olive green
- ⅜ oz (10 g) pomegranate
- ⅜ oz (10 g) butterscotch yellow
- orange mixture:
    - ⅛ oz (5 g) clementine
    - 1/16 oz (2 g) butterscotch
    - 1/16 oz (2 g) white
- ⅛ oz (5 g) white

TOOLS

- wax paper
- nested round and square cookie cutters, such as Kemper Round-Rose Cutters, Kemper Circle Cutters, and Kemper Square Hole Cutters, ranging in size from ⅜" to 1½" (1 to 3.8 cm)
- needle tool
- clay scraper and/or blade
- clay extruder
- toothbrush or stiff-bristled brush
- pencil
- scissors

- ruler
- ⅝" (1.6 cm) circle punch

OTHER MATERIALS

- Bake & Bond Bakeable Adhesive, or white glue
- 5½" x 4¾" (14 x 12.1 cm) metal CD tin
- black acrylic paint
- coordinated solid and patterned *scrapbook paper* for game board and pieces
- white glue
- brown permanent marker
- ten ¼" (6 mm) power magnets
- liquid polymer clay
- resin, such as UV Magic-Glos

QUICK REFERENCE

Scrapbook paper. To start this project, find scrapbook paper in a pattern you like and use it for the game pieces. Then mix your clay to match the colors in the paper. I used Rustic Mustard by the Paper Studio (B11-P-P24) for the solid color and Spicy Circles by Bo-Bunny Press (Shabby Princess Collection) for the game pieces.

How to Cover the Tin

1 Condition the green clay and roll it out to the
pasta machine's fifth-thickest setting. Open
the CD tin. Separate the top and bottom, and set
aside the bottom half. With your fingers or a paper
towel, spread a very light coating of Bake & Bond
adhesive or white glue all over the top and sides of
the top half of the tin. Press the clay onto the tin,
being careful not to trap any air. Fold the clay over
the edges and trim them along the tin's bottom
lip with a clay blade. (An extruded clay border will
cover this, so it doesn't need to be perfect.) Press
and roll a crumpled ball of wax paper on the top of
the tin to texture it.

TIP While you can use any clay brand for this project,
Studio by Sculpey brand works especially well.
It has a non-sticky consistency that makes it less
likely to adhere to itself or the tools, making it easier to
move around for the inlay technique. The fact that the colors
look great straight from the package is a bonus.

1

2

2 Press a 1½" (3.8 cm) (or your largest) circle
cookie cutter into the center of the tin. Cut all
the way through the clay, then remove the cutter
and the clay circle.

3 If the clay circle didn't come out with the
cutter, use a needle tool to scratch lines in
the clay, starting near the circle's edge and pulling
toward the middle. Then scrape under the clay to
pull the shape up and out. Be careful not to disturb
the clay outside the circle, which will remain on
the tin. Remove any small clay crumbs from the
tin's surface, so they won't cause raised areas under
the next inlaid layer. If any crumbs spread to the
surrounding clay, gently press tape or a softened
clay ball onto the crumbs to pick them up. Check
for crumbs regularly to avoid pressing them into
the clay.

3

4 Condition red, orange, yellow, and white clays. Roll each of these and the remaining green clay to the pasta machine's fifth-thickest setting. Working on wax paper, use the same cookie cutter to cut out the first inlay from the yellow clay. Carefully lift this piece with a clay blade or scraper, flexing the wax paper to avoid distorting the shape. Put the yellow circle in the cutout spot in the middle of the tin.

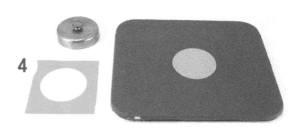

5 Use your finger to smooth the edges of the newly placed shape, pushing the outer edges gently outward so they bind to the surrounding clay without distorting either shape. Use your next-largest cutter to cut a shape out of the center of the tin's yellow circle. Replace the cut-out area with a matching shape cut from a contrasting color. Repeat until you reach the ⅜" (1 cm) circle cutter, or your smallest cutter.

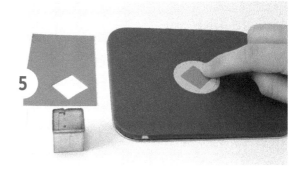

6 For the appliquéd pieces on the surrounding clay, cut out three 1¼" (3.2 cm) circles and three ¾" (1.9 cm) circles from the yellow clay. Apply a small amount of liquid polymer clay to the back of the circles to create a better bond. Place two of the large circles on top of the green clay, laying them down carefully to avoid distortion or air bubbles.

Cut the third large circle in half, and adhere the halves so they appear to go over the tin's edges.

7 Cut two green ¾" (1.9 cm) circles. Cut a ½" (1.3 cm) red circle and a ½" (1.3 cm) white circle. Stack these on top of the yellow circles, adhering with liquid polymer clay.

(continued)

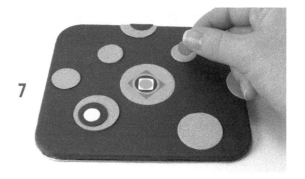

How to Cover the Tin continued

8 Use a needle tool to poke holes around the edges of some of the appliquéd pieces. This adds a stitched look and also helps to attach the appliqué to the clay. A craft knife or a tool with a thin flat head can be used to create a faux straight stitch. Vary the size of the tool and the placement of the stitches for a variety of stitched looks.

9 Make tiny green balls, and place them around an appliqué piece to resemble embroidered French knots. Use a needle tool to apply a tiny drop of liquid polymer clay to either the ball itself or the clay surface.

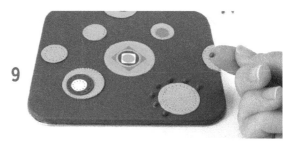

10 Fill the clay extruder's barrel with the remaining green clay. Use the medium circle disk to extrude a border for the tin. Apply liquid polymer clay around the clay on the tin's edges to strengthen the bond. Pull the extruded clay snake around and press it into the liquid polymer clay. Cut the ends of the extruded clay border at an angle and smooth the seam. If desired, add a smaller extruded accent around the design in the tin's center. Bake the tin according to the clay manufacturer's instructions.

11 After the clay has cooled, antique it with black acrylic paint. Use a toothbrush to apply the paint to the clay, focusing on getting the paint into the stitched areas. Only paint one small area at a time to make sure you have time to remove the paint before it stains the lighter-colored surface areas.

12 Wipe the excess paint off the surface, leaving it only in the crevices. If too much paint remains, use a paper towel soaked in rubbing alcohol to scrub off the excess.

How to Make the Game Board

1 To make the game board for the inside of the CD tin, use a pencil to trace around the bottom of the CD tin onto scrapbook paper. Use scissors to cut just inside the traced lines. Try inserting the paper into the bottom to see if it fits; if not, trim the edges as necessary.

2 Use a ruler to mark 2" (5 cm) and 3½" (8.9 cm) lightly with a pencil at the top and bottom of the long side of the tin. Mark 1⅝" (4.1 cm) and 3⅛" (7.9 cm) at the top and bottom of the short side.

3 To draw the tic-tac-toe grid, align a ruler to the dots, and use a brown marker to draw the lines. Stop ½" (1.3 cm) from the edges of the long sides and ⅛" (3 mm) from the edges of the short sides.

4 With your fingers or a paper towel, spread white glue in a thin, even coat in the inside of the bottom half of the tin. Smooth the paper onto the glue.

1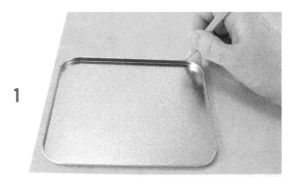

3

4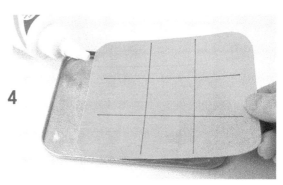

How to Make the Game Pieces

1 Cut a strip of scrapbook paper large enough to make ten ⅝" (1.6 cm) round tiles. Place the paper face-up on your baking surface, then spread a thin layer of liquid polymer clay so it covers the surface of the paper. Place the paper in the oven and bake according to the liquid polymer clay manufacturer's instructions.

2 Allow the coated paper to cool, then peel it off the baking surface. Trim off any excess liquid polymer clay with scissors. Use a ⅝" (1.3 cm) circle punch to make ten circles.

3 Roll the red and green clay into sheets at the pasta machine's thickest setting. Use a ¾" (1.9 cm) round cookie cutter to cut out five red circles and five green circles. Roll the remaining clay to the fourth-thickest setting, then cut out five more circles of each color.

Add a drop of liquid polymer clay to the top of each clay circle. Place the coated circle of paper onto the glue, centered on the clay disk.

4 Turn the game piece upside-down. Use a ⅜" (1 cm) round cutter to punch a hole in the middle of the back. Replace the clay you remove with one of the power magnets.

1

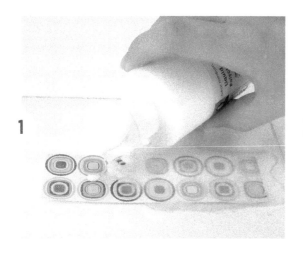

3

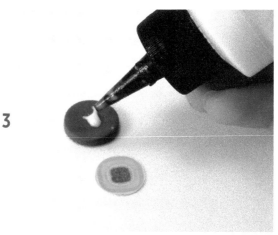

2

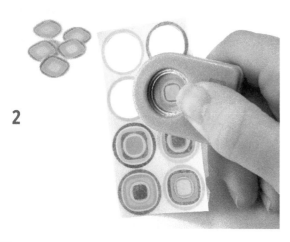

4

5 Use liquid polymer clay to glue one of the matching thin clay circles onto the game piece's back side, hiding the magnet inside.

6 Smooth the seams on the sides of the game piece. Push the top edges of the clay up to hide the paper's edges and give the game piece a more rounded look.

7 Repeat the steps to make ten game pieces, five of each color. As you finish each piece, place it on a baking tile at least a couple of inches (5 cm) from the next one. Placing the uncured game pieces too close together may cause the magnets to attract each other and distort the uncured clay. Bake the game pieces according to the clay manufacturer's instructions.

8 Allow the game pieces to cool without removing them from the tile. Add a few drops of Magic-Glos UV Resin to the top of each piece. Use a heat gun to disperse any bubbles, then cure in full sun or under a UV lamp for 10 to 15 minutes. (See pages 148 and 149 for more information on using Magic-Glos.)

5

6

8

Variations

This variation uses polymer clay faux wood techniques to cover a papier mâché box for a more traditional inlay look.

Mosaic Clock

Polymer clay is an ideal material for mosaic making. The tiles can be any size, shape, and color, plus they're easy to cut before or after baking—no more scoring or nipping! With polymer clay, mosaic artists don't have to be limited by the selection of tiles available to them.

This clock project will show how to cut the tiles, lay them out, and add grout. Once you understand the basics, it's fun to change things up. Try texturing or stamping tiles, or even transferring images onto them. You can carefully map out your mosaic pattern using grid paper or a computer spreadsheet, or you can randomize tile placement by drawing tiles from a sack.

WHAT YOU'LL LEARN...

- How to create even polymer clay tiles and half-tiles
- How to create a sturdy lightweight clay base for the clock
- How to lay out mosaic tiles
- How to grout using a clay mixture

WHAT YOU'LL NEED...

CLAY

- Studio by Sculpey or clay of choice:
- dark green mixture:
    - ⅜ oz (10 g) patina
    - ⅙ oz (5 g) after midnight (black)
- light green:
    - ⅜ oz (10 g) patina
- dark rose mixture:
    - ⅙ oz (5 g) Sedona
    - ³⁄₃₂ oz (2.5 g) dark green mixture
- light rose mixture:
    - ³⁄₃₂ oz (2.5 g) whipped cream
    - ³⁄₃₂ oz (2.5 g) dark rose mixture
- ¼ oz (7 g) whipped cream
- ¼ oz (7 g) after midnight
- 4 Tbsp (about the equivalent of a 2-ounce clay package) Sculpey UltraLight (white)

TOOLS

- square ⅜" (1 cm) Kemper cutter
- large ceramic tile(s)
- ruler
- clay extruder
- brayer or acrylic roller, optional

OTHER MATERIALS

- index card
- liquid polymer clay
- clock mechanism kit (¼" [6 mm] deep)
- wooden craft stick
- paper towels
- rubbing alcohol
- Sculpey Clay Softener

How to Make a Mosaic Clock

1 Condition the dark green, light green, dark rose, and light rose clays. Roll out each color to the pasta machine's third-thickest setting. Working on a large ceramic tile or other bakeable surface, press each colored sheet onto the tile so it sticks in place. Use a ⅜" (1 cm) square cutter to punch out forty dark green, fifteen light green, three dark rose, and five light rose squares. Punch firmly enough to cut through the clay, but try to leave the clay squares stuck to the ceramic tile. Once you have cut out all the squares of one color, peel back the surrounding clay sheet and set it aside. Bake the clay squares according to the clay manufacturer's instructions.

TIP You don't have to use a square cutter for tiles. Use a regular or polymer clay ruler to measure and mark lines in the clay sheet, then cut them out with your clay blade.

2 Condition the white and black clay, and roll them out to the pasta machine's third-thickest setting. Place the sheets on a ceramic tile as before, but press down an index card onto the clay sheet before you cut any squares. Line the edge of the cutter up against the index card to cut each square, using the card as a guide. Pull up the surrounding clay sheet.

3 Press down the clay blade into the middle of the squares, cutting the whole row of squares in half with a single cut. Bake the half squares.

4 Condition the Sculpey UltraLight clay, and roll it out to the pasta machine's thickest setting. Use a clay blade to cut the sheet to a 4" (10.2 cm) square. Find the center of the clay sheet by using the dull edge of your clay blade to press in lines from each corner to the opposite corner. The spot where the lines meet is the middle. Place the nut from the clock mechanism kit there, and run a knife around the inside of the nut to cut a hole through the clay. Bake this sheet according to Sculpey UltraLight's baking instructions.

5 Spread a layer of liquid polymer clay along the bottom edge of the clock base, covering a large enough area to lay the first row of tiles. Start by placing the corner pieces, leaving a little extra space for grout around the outer edge. Use a ruler to find the middle of the row, then center the middle tile there. Fill in the remaining spots of the first row with tiles.

6 Continue spreading adhesive and laying down tiles, working from the outside edges toward the middle. When you place the half-tiles, follow the existing grout lines while leaving a small amount of space between each half. Alternate the directions the halves are facing for emphasis. Bake the clock to adhere the tiles.

(continued)

TIP Sculpey UltraLight is lighter than regular clays, which makes it a good choice for larger projects like wall hangings. It is also an inexpensive option when you are using large amounts. It bonds well with clay and liquid polymer clay, which makes it a good choice for projects that need an armature or base.

Because Sculpey UltraLight has a different texture than many clays, it can be difficult to run though a pasta machine. If you have trouble, you can use a brayer or acrylic roller instead. You could also try mixing the UltraLight half and half with regular clay for a firmer consistency. If you're handy with a drill, a wood base would work well instead of the clay base—just bake it in the oven at clay temperatures first to remove excess moisture.

5

6

Mosaic Clock *continued*

7 Mix the leftover Sculpey UltraLight with a small amount of patina clay and a couple squirts of Clay Softener to make a very soft clay *grout*.

Spread liquid polymer clay into the gaps between the tiles, then use your fingers to press a generous amount of the grout mixture around and between the tiles.

7

8 Drag a craft stick across the top of the mosaic to scrape away the excess grout. After each pass, wipe the stick off with a paper towel. Remove the bulk of the excess grout this way.

9 Use a dry paper towel to firmly wipe the remaining grout off the surface. Pour a little rubbing alcohol on the paper towel to clean off any final spots. Run a needle tool around inside of the circle in the center to clean out excess grout.

8

QUICK REFERENCE

Grout. The grout color really impacts the look of the finished mosaic, so test your color by rolling thin clay ropes and placing them on top of the tiles. A lighter colored grout will make the tile colors look lighter, while a dark grout will do the opposite.

9

10 Place the leftover dark green clay in the clay extruder, and use the small flat disk to press out a long thin border. Add liquid polymer clay to the outer edge of the clock, and attach the extruded border. Smooth the cut ends together with your finger. Bake the mosaic.

11 Follow the instructions in the clock mechanism kit to assemble the clock. If the center hole is too small, run a craft knife around the circle to widen it slightly.

10

11

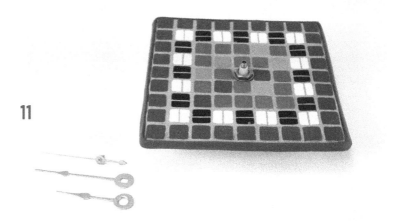

Variations

This vessel was formed on the outside of a 2½" (6.4 cm) cookie cutter. The tiles on top were cut freehand, while the smaller tiles on the side were punched with a square hole punch from thin baked sheets of clay.

The butterfly often forgets it once was a caterpillar.

Toner Transfer and Tear-Away Technique Artist Trading Card

Image transfers are a handy way to add text, photos, and other images to your artwork. Using just a computer and a printer or copier, you can customize your clay piece with words, poems, or sayings printed in your favorite font. Artist Trading Cards (ATCs) are 2½" x 3½" (6.4 x 8.9 cm) works of art that are created and traded by artists around the world. Because of their small size, ATCs are a fun way to experiment with different techniques. This ATC demonstrates two different techniques: a toner transfer for the text, and a tear-away technique for the image. Both of these techniques require toner-based printouts from either a laser printer or a toner photocopy machine. The toner transfer will transfer the ink from the text onto the card. The tear-away technique will do just the opposite: the toner ink will bind to the top layer of clay, leaving an imprint of the image when the paper and clay are quickly ripped away.

WHAT YOU'LL LEARN...

- How to make a simplified faux ivory
- How to do the tear-away technique
- How to do a basic toner transfer using the oven method

WHAT YOU'LL NEED...

CLAY

- Studio by Sculpey or clay of choice:
- cream mixture:
    - ⅛ oz (4 g) ecru
    - ½ oz (14 g) translucent
- ½ oz (14 g) white
- ½ oz (14 g) translucent

TOOLS

- ceramic tile or other baking surface
- bone folder or credit card for burnishing
- heat embossing gun

- timer
- scissors
- toothbrush or stiff-bristled brush

OTHER MATERIALS

- royalty-free image (image shown comes from *Merian's Antique Botanical Prints* by Dover Publications)
- laser printer or toner photocopier
- card stock
- brown acrylic paint
- paper towels
- rubbing alcohol

Tear-Away Technique

1 Find a royalty-free image approximately 2½" wide by 3" (6.4 × 7.6 cm) tall, or resize an image on your computer to this size. Print the image on cardstock, using the darkest and highest quality ink options your laser printer or toner-based photocopier offers. Cut out the image, folding down one corner to use as a pull-tab later.

2 Condition the white, translucent, and cream clay mixture thoroughly. Stretch each color of clay into a snake about 3" (7.6 cm) long, and place the snakes side by side.

3 Twist the three snakes together in your hand to create stripes of color. As you twist and roll the log, it will get longer. Once it's about twice its original length, fold it in half and start twisting it again. Continue until the stripes are fairly close together.

4 Your log should be approximately 3" (7.6 cm) long (fold it in half again if it's much longer than this). Flatten the log slightly, then put it through the pasta machine's thickest setting with the long edge touching the rollers. The resulting sheet needs to be at least 2½" × 3½" (6.4 × 7.6 cm); roll it through at the second-thickest setting if necessary to reach this size. Find the section of the sheet with the best pattern, and cut around that section to create a clay sheet 2½" wide by 3½" tall (6.4 × 7.6 cm). Place the clay on a ceramic tile or other oven-safe surface.

5 Place the image facedown on your clay sheet, and use a bone folder or the edge of a credit card to burnish it. Make sure there are no air bubbles trapped between the paper and clay.

6 Use a heat embossing gun to heat the back of the transfer for 15 to 20 seconds. Move the heat gun constantly, keeping it a couple of inches (5 cm) above the clay. If the edges of the paper start to curl up, burnish them down. Set a timer for five minutes and allow the clay and transfer to sit.

7 After five minutes, grasp the turned-up tab between your thumb and forefinger. In one quick motion, pull your hand across to rip the paper from the clay. The top layer of clay should have stuck to the toner on the card stock, leaving a shallow impression in the clay everywhere the toner was touching it.

TIP Many factors affect tear-away technique success. Try these suggestions if you're having trouble:
• Some image software packages offer a "Photocopy" filter. Use this to darken and simplify the lines of your image.

• Gray inks don't tear away as well as dark black inks. If you have a laser printer that offers an option of printing in black or color ink, select black.

• Fresh printouts work better than those that are several days old. Heavier paper works better than lightweight copy paper.

• Warm, well-conditioned clay works best for this technique. White and very light colors work better than highly pigmented colors. Certain brands, such as Studio by Sculpey, may also give better results.

• If you find that the ink transfers instead of tearing away, vary the length of time you allow the clay to sit after heating the ink.

• If all else fails, pick at areas that didn't tear away with a needle tool to give it a dotted effect. You could also use a failed tear-away attempt as an excuse to try your carving skills (see "Carving" page 158).

Toner Transfer Technique

1 Use word processing software to type up a quote using any favorite font (example uses Adler in a dark brown) in bold. Print in reverse or mirror image using the highest quality print option available. Print on either regular copy paper or cardstock.

Cut out the image close to the edges of the text on three sides, but leave a border on one side to use as a pull-tab.

2 Press the paper facedown on the bottom area of the clay sheet. Burnish using a bone folder or your fingers to ensure there are no trapped air bubbles. Place the card, with the paper still in place, in the toaster oven and set a timer for five minutes.

1

2

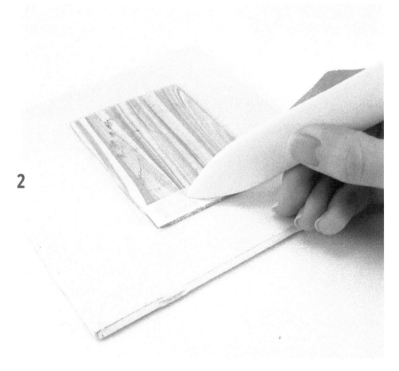

3 Gently pull the transfer off from one side to the other. The ink should be transferred to the clay. Place the card back in the oven and allow it to finish baking.

3

4 Apply brown acrylic paint to the torn-away sections with a toothbrush or stiff-bristled brush. Wipe away paint on the surface with a dry paper towel. Pour a little rubbing alcohol on a paper towel to wipe away excess paint.

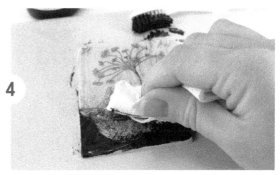

4

TIP Smooth the clay sheet onto the baking surface before applying the toner image transfer. This can help prevent the paper from curling and pulling up the edges of the clay. If you still have problems with curling, try putting a tile on top of the clay piece as it bakes. Use an index card between the clay and tile to prevent shiny spots.

Don't allow the transfer to bake longer than 5 to 7 minutes initially, or the paper may stick to the clay and cause cracking when it is removed.

Peel the transfer slowly from the side, otherwise you may end up inadvertently doing the tear-away technique.

If there are small areas that didn't transfer, touch them up with matching acrylic paint or clay-compatible permanent marker after marking.

Variations

This ATC shows another example of the tear-away technique. After baking, the butterfly was antiqued with black paint, then the card was covered with alcohol inks.

Artist Trading Card

By: ..Angela..Mabray.............

Date: 2/..24../..2010...........

E-m............@craftygnat..com

T-Shirt Transfer Artist Trading Card

If you have an ink-jet printer, you can use T-shirt transfer paper to create beautiful transfers with deeply saturated colors. Be sure to buy the Avery T-Shirt Transfer Paper for Light Fabrics, since the transfer paper for dark fabrics creates a decal instead of a transfer. (On the other hand, a decal might be the perfect thing for a particular project!) Transfer papers can be expensive, so always do a test print first on a regular sheet of paper. You can also save money by placing as many images as possible on the page before printing.

WHAT YOU'LL LEARN

- How to do an image transfer using T-shirt transfer paper
- How to apply pearl powders to uncured polymer clay

WHAT YOU'LL NEED

CLAY

- light gold mixture:

    ¼ oz (7 g) ecru

    ¼ oz (7 g) gold

- dark gold mixture:

    ½ oz (14 g) black

    ¼ oz (7 g) gold

TOOLS

- ceramic tile or other baking surface
- craft knife and/or clay blade
- bone folder or credit card for burnishing
- timer
- scissors
- toothbrush or stiff-bristled brush
- clay extruder
- small paintbrush

OTHER MATERIALS

- royalty-free image (image shown comes from *Full-Color Old-Time Label Art* by Dover Publications)
- Avery T-Shirt Transfer Paper for Light Fabrics
- liquid polymer clay
- Sunset Gold Pearl Ex powder, or other pearl powder
- Studio by Sculpey Glossy Glaze or other clay-compatible glaze

How to Make a T-Shirt Transfer ATC

1 Select an image and resize it to no more than 2½" (6.4 cm) wide. Use an ink-jet printer to print the image on Avery T-Shirt Transfer Paper for Light Fabrics. Be sure to use the printer's highest print quality settings and select reverse or mirror image if the image includes any text.

Cut out the transfer. Leave very little border except in one spot, where you'll fold back the paper to create a pull-tab.

TIP Using others' artwork may infringe on copyrights, so stick to sources such as these:

• Dover Publications publishes books full of royalty-free images with a wide variety of themes.

• Some Flickr users offer their photos under Creative Commons licenses (check the license type to make sure it matches your desired use). The Library of Congress also offers many public domain photos on their Flickr photostream, though they advise you to check individual photos to verify there are no restrictions.

• Your own photos and drawings, or your children's artwork, make for truly original image transfers.

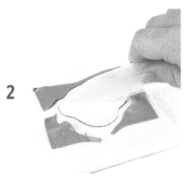

2 Condition the light gold clay mixture and roll it out to a medium thickness on the pasta machine. The sheet should be at least as large as the image you want to transfer. Press the clay sheet onto the tile, eliminating any air bubbles. Press the transfer paper image-side down on top of the clay sheet. Trace around the transfer with a craft knife to cut the clay sheet down to size. Burnish with a bone folder or your fingers to eliminate any air bubbles between the transfer paper and the clay.

Place the clay in the toaster oven with the transfer paper still on top, and set a timer for five minutes. It may help to place a tile on top of the transfer while it is in the oven to prevent the paper from curling.

3 Use the tab you created to slowly pull the transfer from one edge to the other. The image should have transferred to the clay. Place the clay back in the oven to finish baking.

4 Condition the dark gold clay mixture, mixing in any leftover light gold clay mixture. Roll this clay to a medium thickness on the pasta machine. Cut the sheet down to 2½" wide by 3½" tall (6.4 × 8.9 cm) and place it on a ceramic tile or other oven-safe work surface. Texture the clay with a toothbrush or stiff-bristled brush.

5 Once the image transfer has cured and cooled, use liquid polymer clay to adhere it approximately in the middle of the clay sheet. Apply liquid polymer clay to the top of the transfer, too, as this will make the transfer waterproof.

Put the leftover gold clay in the extruder, and press out clay snakes using the twelve-hole medium extruder disk. Twist two snakes together to make a frame for the transfer. Repeat to make a border for the edge of the card.

6 Decorate the remaining background area with extruded clay shaped into S curves and other decorative swirls and shapes. Slice ⅛" (3 mm) pieces off of one of the extruded snakes, then roll between your fingers to create balls that are all the same size. Dip the balls into a small amount of liquid polymer clay before placing them on the background.

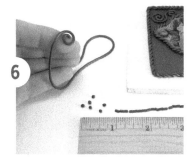

TIP If you're attaching uncured clay to cured clay, always use liquid polymer clay to act as a glue between them. Uncured clay may bind to other uncured clay pieces without any additional adhesive, especially when both pieces are warm and well-conditioned. Very small pieces, such as the clay balls on this card, may fall off if they don't have adhesive. It never hurts to add a little liquid polymer clay to create an extra-strong bond.

7 Once all the embellishments are in place, use pearl powders to highlight the raised areas of the design. Rub a small amount of the powder on the extruded clay borders and swirls with your fingertip. If excess powder falls on the background, you can use a piece of tape to pick it up, or you can leave it there to add to the distressed look of the piece. Bake the card according to the clay manufacturer's instructions.

8 When the card has cooled, use a small paintbrush to apply glaze to the raised areas. This will protect the pearl powders and add a little extra shine.

Glossary

Acrylic roller: A clear rod that can be used instead of a pasta machine to roll out sheets of polymer clay.

Antiquing: Applying paint to a polymer clay surface, then wiping most of it off, so it remains just in the crevices of the design.

Appliqué: Any small pieces of polymer clay applied to the top of a larger piece. Originally a quilting technique.

Baking: Placing the clay in the oven to harden it. Baking times and temperatures vary by brand. Also called curing.

Baking surface: An oven-safe surface, such as an index card or ceramic tile, used to place the polymer clay piece in the oven for curing.

Cabochon: A domed piece of clay with a flat back. A clay cabochon can be treated like a stone cabochon in that it can be set with a bezel of clay or beads.

Cane: A design, sometimes very intricate, that runs all the way through a clay log. Slices are cut off the end to reveal the design.

Clay blade: Thin, very sharp blade used to cut through clay. In addition to the standard rigid blades, flexible blades and wavy blades are also available.

Conditioning: Working the clay to soften it and combine its ingredients. Clay can be conditioned by hand, or by using tools like a pasta machine or food processor.

Curing: Causing the clay to harden by baking it according to the manufacturer's instructions.

Extruder: Tool that presses clay through one of a variety of disks to create shaped clay snakes.

Glaze: A material used to protect the clay surface and/or add shine. It's best to use glazes that have been tested with clay, as some glazes will react with clay over time.

Image transfer: Copying a printed image onto clay using one of a variety of techniques.

Inlay: The placement of smaller decorative elements in indented areas of a larger piece. Originally a woodworking technique.

Leaching: Placing clay between sheets of paper to remove excess plasticizer. This technique helps make a soft clay more firm.

Liquid polymer clay: Polymer clay product useful for gluing or glazing polymer clay, or as a transfer medium. Usually refers to a translucent liquid, although some brands also offer opaque tinted versions.

Marbling: Partially mixing two or more colors together to achieve a marblelike effect.

Metal leaf: A very thin sheet of colored metal that can be applied to clay for a gilded effect. Often called gold leaf or silver leaf, although metal leaf does not actually contain these precious metals.

Mica shift: A technique used with pearl or metallic clays. The mica particles in the clay are first lined up in one direction, then some are displaced by stamping or other methods. The technique gives an illusion of depth to the clay.

Mokume-Gane: Pressing items into stacked sheets of polymer clay, then cutting off slices to reveal the pattern inside. Originally a metalworking technique.

Mold: A tool made from one of a variety of materials (such as silicone molding compound or polymer clay). Used with polymer clay to create replicas of a sculpture or texture.

Pasta machine: A tool originally used to flatten sheets of dough for pasta-making. The pasta machine is ideal for conditioning polymer clay and rolling out flat, even sheets in a variety of thicknesses. Polymer clay companies now manufacture clay conditioning machines specifically intended for use with polymer clay.

Phthalate: A plasticizer previously used in many brands of polymer clay. Most manufacturers have reformulated their clays to eliminate the use of phthalates in response to health concerns.

Plasticizer: A substance added to clay to keep it soft until it is cured.

Release agent: Any material used to prevent clay from sticking to a mold, texture sheet, or other surface. Examples of release agents include water, corn starch, or pearl powders.

Sanding/buffing: Finishing technique used by many polymer clay artists. Sanding eliminates imperfections, and buffing creates a shiny surface without the need for glazes.

Scrap clay: Clay left over from a project, such as the ends of canes. If the mixed-together color of the scrap clay doesn't appeal to you, use it in hidden areas like the center of cane-covered beads.

Scraper: Thin sheet of oval-shaped aluminum. Often used to move uncured clay sheets from one surface to another.

Skinner blend: Technique where the clay is fed through the pasta machine repeatedly to create gradient-blended sheets of color. Judith Skinner is credited with creating this technique.

Surgeon's knot: An overhand knot with the end of the string going through the knot loop twice before pulling tight.

Work surface: Any smooth flat surface used for polymer clay work. Good options include ceramic, marble, glass, or wax paper.

Resources

Supplies

Many local craft stores carry polymer clay supplies. The following retail and manufacturer websites can supply specialty products mentioned in this book that may not be available locally:

Polymer Clay Express
www.polymerclayexpress.com
Kemper cutters, ShadeTex texture plates, Kato Liquid Polyclay, Ranger embossing powders, Pearl Ex powders, Speedball carving tools, Marxit, heat embossing tools, punches, CD tins, business card cases

The Clay Alley
www.clayalley.com
Kemper cutters, ShadeTex texture plates, Kato Liquid Polyclay, and Marxit

Boston Craftworks
www.polymerclayprojects.com
Business card cases, clock kits, Amazing Twist Pens, Kato Liquid Polyclay, and Pearl Ex Powders

Makin's Clay
www.makinsclay.com
Clay extruder

Alumilite
www.amazingmoldputty.com
Amazing Mold Putty

Lisa Pavelka
www.lisapavelka.com
Magic-Glos UV resin

Polyform
www.sculpey.com
Sculpey, Premo!, and Studio by Sculpey products and tools

Dover Publications
www.doverpublications.com
Royalty-free image books

More Sites of Interest

Swap-Bot (www.swap-bot.com): Join swaps for Artist Trading Cards and more.

International Polymer Clay Association (www.npcg.org): Find polymer clay information for local and international artists.

Polymer Clay Daily (www.polymerclaydaily.com): Get inspired by the artistic possibilities of polymer clay.

About the Authors

Angela Mabray first happened upon polymer clay in a toy store. While she quickly realized it wasn't just for kids, she still feels a childlike joy each time she finds something new to do with polymer clay. Angela lives with her husband and son in Oklahoma, where she co-founded the Central Oklahoma Polymer Clay Guild. She is also a member of the International Polymer Clay Association. Her polymer clay projects have appeared in Polymer Café, on HGTV's *That's Clever* show, and on many blogs. She writes about polymer clay at www.craftygoat.com.

Kim Otterbein has had a love for beads all her life and still has a baggie of seed beads from the 1960s. Kim's training as a textile designer and painter seems to blend right in with jewelry making. Kim is the primary teacher for classes and workshops at the Bead House in Bristol, Rhode Island, sharing her wide range of knowledge and experience in beading, knotting, wire wrapping, and polymer clay. She is a certified instructor of Precious Metal Clay (PMC) and also a silversmith. She has had many projects and instructional articles published in various magazines, including *Bead & Button, Belle Armoire, Art Jewelry, Beadwork, Polymer Café,* and *Lapidary Journal.* To see her work, go to www.thebeadhouse.com and click on KO Design.

Index

CPSIA information can be obtained
at www.ICGtesting.com
Printed in the USA
LVHW070346261120
672679LV00023B/3058